first steps
in counselling

first steps in counselling

ursula o'farrell

VERITAS

First published 1988 by
Veritas Publications
7–8 Lower Abbey Street
Dublin 1, Ireland
Email publications@veritas.ie
Website www.veritas.ie

This edition published 2006

A catalogue record for this book is available from the British Library.

ISBN 1 85390 919 X

10 9 8 7 6 5 4 3 2

British Library Cataloguing
in Publication Data.
A catalogue record for
this book is available
from the British Library.

Cover design by Michael O'Farrell
Printed in the Republic of Ireland by ColourBooks Ltd, Dublin

*Veritas books are printed on paper made from the wood pulp of managed forests. For every
tree felled, at least one tree is planted, thereby renewing natural resources.*

To Mary Ryan of St Patrick's College, Maynooth,
who has encouraged and sustained so many of us involved
in counselling today with her vision, her warmth,
and her constant good humour.

Contents

Introduction

Counselling is today widely accepted as a valuable form of help for people in distress. In response to the increased demand for counselling services, there has been a corresponding growth in training courses for counsellors in Ireland, as well as in the provision of different categories of counselling, such as addiction, family, bereavement, relationships. Counsellors are being sought for medical practices, for court and probation referrals, for hospitals and health boards.

The trend of treating the whole person rather than just the problem they present continues, and in medicine, business, education, etc. counselling is seen either as a useful addition to primary expertise or as a specific additional qualification to be used within a particular work setting. Trained professional counsellors are working within employment assistance programmes, the gardaí, schools, and many voluntary organisations.

The Irish Association for Counselling and Psychotherapy (IACP) has become an integral part of the counselling profession in Ireland, setting standards for training and practitioners, providing information for members of the public about the services available, offering a referral service for its accredited membership, encouraging research and writing, and maintaining links with our counterparts abroad.

Despite this growth and recognition, the fundamental importance of the relationship between the client and the counsellor has not changed, and the task of the counsellor is still concerned with the development of that relationship and its process from initial contact to effective outcome. I have tried here to outline the basic requirements of that relationship, and to look at how the counsellor can responsibly create a climate of acceptance and safety, within which fundamental trust can grow and the client can risk making changes.

Chapter 1 looks at the use of counselling skills in our daily life and at work, and discusses counselling in Ireland. Chapter 2 outlines different approaches to counselling and psychotherapy. The attributes and skills necessary for effective counselling are discussed in chapters 3 and 4, and chapters 5 and 6 deal with the development of the counselling process. Self-awareness and the need for emotional strength and stability are the themes of chapter 7, and chapter 8 consists of a brief look at the two somewhat different aspects of group counselling and crisis counselling. Chapter 9 looks beyond the practical issues to our limitations and our reasons for counselling, the ethical nature and the confidentiality of the relationship, and the outcomes looked for by our clients.

This book, therefore, is an outline of some of the basic requirements for those who are aware of the value of counselling and who would like to know more about its theory and practice. It is important, however, that the reader be aware that, while trying to be objective, my attitudes, values and personal philosophy will underline much of what I have written. My approach is person-centred and based on the theories of Carl Rogers, emphasising the self-responsibility of the client. In many instances in this book, only this single approach is presented. Also, despite the many changes in the counselling field, and in my own life over the years, I am still sustained by the belief that God is taking care of my clients and myself.

Ursula O'Farrell

1. What is Counselling?

AIMS

One of the difficulties of writing about a profession in the process of becoming established is that, although some basic terms have become widely accepted, many others were adopted in the earlier writings and may no longer have their original meanings. Even the words 'counsellor' and 'client' have been put aside by some writers as too confining and legalistic, and have been replaced by 'helper' and 'helpee'. However, it is necessary to have a clear idea of the meaning of the work we are doing, and perhaps it is good to start with the concept of counselling as based on change: change of perspective, of circumstances, of behaviour, of coping ability. If people are not satisfied with their lives as they are, they look for a different tomorrow. They are searching for change.

Contrary to a popular perception of counselling, the task of the counsellor is not to advise people about their choice of action. We usually do not have sufficient knowledge of this person to make important decisions for them. We listen and explore with our clients, we highlight some of the shared material and we support their choices.

The counsellor helps the client to identify choices for the future and supports their implementation. If the desired changes do not lie within the client's capability, then these are not viable choices. The aim of the counsellor is to help clients recognise how they would realistically like their lives to be, and then help them to actualise or achieve these aims. In a situation which cannot be changed, for example when someone close to our client has died, then the change consists of *adjusting* to the new circumstances.

COUNSELLING SKILLS IN DAILY LIFE

It is difficult to realise how often we use counselling skills in our family settings, in our communities, at work or in casual meetings on the street. When we are aware of what another person is really saying and really meaning underneath bold or brave words, when we can see beyond faltering attempts at communication, we are using these skills. In whatever setting we work, listening with all our senses will help us to read between the emotional lines being expressed. We will see beyond the anger of the dying person to the fear they cannot express, recognise the cheeky bravado of the adolescent as merely a cloak for uncertainty in the face of tomorrow, and identify the indifference of the alcoholic as a defence against self-loathing, which could destroy him.

We often respond automatically to the expressed defences of other people. If someone shouts at me, I may react to the loud words. Learning to look for the reasons why this person is angry places the emphasis on understanding rather than on merely reacting. The attributes required in order to be an effective counsellor – unconditional positive regard, accurate empathy and genuineness – are part of loving our neighbour. Learning to be a better counsellor makes us more tolerant, more understanding, more charitable.

The application of these attributes and skills is perhaps easier in a counselling or healing situation than, for example, in our family setting, where reactions become automatic. Familiar with those around us, we no longer see or understand the responses they trigger in us. The real meaning behind a statement such as 'You're always coming in late' may be quite different from what is actually heard by the person to whom it is said. The automatic reaction of the listener may be to get angry at the accusations, at the injustice of the word 'always' which is probably untrue, and to rebel against the judgement or criticism implied in 'late' (late for what? late by whose standards?). So tempers flare and rows ensue, piling up further resentment for the next 'You're always coming in late'. The use of counselling skills will enable us to recognise our anger and rebellion as automatic responses to an accusation, and to move *out* from our own selves towards the other person to see his pent-up resentment or worry as the real cause of his anger. This ability is basic to all counselling. It demands that we know ourselves, our emotions, our triggers to anger, love and sadness, and far from merely suspending or repressing these when dealing with others, we can actually move beyond our own personal dimension towards the dimension of another.

In everyday communication within many families, the dangerous areas of relationships and loving are often left untouched. These areas are unknown and deep-rooted, and fears and worries are channelled into safer areas such as food, meal-times, time-keeping. When there is some emotional upheaval, or when these fears and anxieties become excessive, the familiar methods of surface communication are no longer sufficient to deal with the crisis. There are several alternatives: to explode in rage and anger, to retreat even further into oneself, to exit from the scene. Alternatively it is possible to emerge from behind the emotional façade to make a positive expression towards the other person, refusing to react in the accustomed way. This kind of bridging movement can result in real communication, by acknowledging the underlying feelings of resentment or fear. How much better to achieve this reality in calmer times!

COUNSELLING AS PART OF OUR WORK
Counselling skills can be useful in the context of our everyday lives, but it is obviously a different situation when we are using these skills in our work, as part of our helping interactions with people in distress. Here it is useful to differentiate between those who are counsellors and those who use counselling skills as part of their further expertise, such as lawyers, the gardaí, nurses, doctors, etc.

The counsellor, trained in the areas of human personality, motivation, growth, and in the practice of counselling skills, is focusing her whole professional person on a client, or clients, and whatever model she is using, whatever the presenting problem of the client, her skills of listening and attending are the loom on which the counsellor-client relationship is woven. This relationship is the therapeutic tool, and the immediate constant use of counselling skills will decide the outcome. However, there is a category of helpers for whom counselling is not their primary focus, but whose work involves listening and attending to the welfare of others. The quality of their work can be enhanced by the knowledge and use of counselling skills. These could include a flight attendant recognising signs of stress in a passenger, a child-care worker correctly interpreting the relationship between a mother and child, or a personnel officer linking isolated incidents at work to a possible drink problem in an employee.

Wherever one is operating on this continuum of counselling, the constant will be the style and philosophy of the person who is counselling. The variables will be the needs and requirements of the client or clients, the constraints of time, commitment, type of problem, realistic outcomes, etc. The need for specialist information will occur in instances of specific problems where a further expertise will be required. For example, in the case of addiction counselling, specialised knowledge of the effects of addiction are essential to effective help.

In all these areas, it is possible to enlist the client on his own behalf, to call on his insight and courage to make the desired changes. Counselling is never something we do to another person. It is an ongoing process, and our intervention of perhaps an hour a week may be crucial, but it is never the whole story. While not with the counsellor, the client is learning to cope and to survive, and while the beginning of change may have come from the counselling sessions, living that change or trying to implement it is the constant work of the client. In the final analysis, the responsibility for change and growth rests firmly on the shoulders of the client, and no counsellor can take it from him.

> An additional reason for focusing on personal responsibility is that virtually every psychological theory either explicitly or implicitly attests to its importance.[1]

This recognition of personal responsibility demands another kind of detachment, in addition to the necessity of not becoming emotionally over-involved. If a person insists on a course of action of which we might personally disapprove, or from which we expect unhappiness for them, then this is their right of personal choice. Basically, people do what they want to do. In counselling, or indeed in any helping situation, it is often possible to discern that someone has made a choice of action because it appears to be the only choice. Offering other ways of looking at the situation, making available more information, may result in a different decision, or may not. But the result is that the client feels there is an element of choice, that there is an alternative. This ability to *choose* can often change, not the course of action, but the effect of it and the climate in which action is taken. To put it simply, a person confined to a wheelchair as a result of an accident or a stroke has a range of things he can no longer do, and also a number of things that he can still do. The element of choice would be on which set he would choose to build, and the quality of his life depends on that choice.

<small>DIFFERENT HELPING AREAS</small>
Counselling takes place in response to an individual's need to identify problem areas, to examine the demands imposed by these, and to find new ways of coping. When the needs of a person are unclear, when the signs and symptoms are all that the person can see (stress, anxiety, etc.), then they may not go to a counsellor. They may approach any one of a large range of people for help, and the presentation of their unhappiness and stress will vary according to their perception of the other person's function as helper. They may go to a doctor, for medicine to ease the headache symptom of distress; to a friend, to whom the background or local colour of the problem is familiar; to a priest or nun, if they see their difficulties as originating in the religious field; to a nurse, to a physiotherapist or occupational therapist, as someone already spending time with the person, who may be seen as having a key to further relieving distress or solving the problem.

The presentation of the basic problem will vary considerably, depending on the perceived role of the person from whom help is sought. For example, a woman, married for twenty years and with three children in their late teens, may be feeling useless and unloved in her role as wife and mother. Seeking help to deal with her misery and unhappiness, she may go to the doctor. If, however, she perceives the doctor's function as healer of bodily pains only, she may only describe physical symptoms such as headaches, and despite the best efforts of the doctor, she may not be able to confide further within this perceived doctor-patient role. If she goes to a friend, she may be cautious in her presentation of facts, perhaps because she does not want to put her friendship at risk by admitting what she sees as her failure, or because she may not want to prejudice her friend against her husband by revealing his indifference to her. Similar censoring might be applied to the other categories of helper, perhaps the idea that a dutiful approach to her difficulties is necessary when presenting them to a 'religious' person, or an imposition of brevity due to an awareness of time constraints when with a professional who is concentrated on a physical aspect of helping. Thanks to increased media discussion, the concept of counselling is not as threatening as it used to be. The perceived 'stigma' of going to a counsellor or therapist has lessened greatly over the past twenty years. It is generally recognised that help is available for personal dilemmas and difficulties, and availing of that help is more acceptable. Clients are becoming aware of the nature of counselling and are less likely to say 'I need you to solve my problem'. A more typical comment today is 'I know you cannot give me answers and solutions but ...'. Being thus familiar with the *concept* of counselling, the reality of the work is less fearful and less strange, and clients are able to enter the relationship with more confidence. They are often knowledgeable about theories and practice, and may ask searching and informed questions about the counsellor's role (which can be threatening to inexperienced counsellors!). However, the perceived role of the helper does colour the nature and extent of disclosure, and it can be very difficult to see beyond this filtered reality to the real truth.

Depending on our audience, our account of an experience or episode in our lives will probably contain a different emphasis, different shadings and meanings. Our truthful description of an accident will probably be different when given to our families, to work colleagues, to the police. The counsellor, or the person using counselling skills, somehow has to step beyond this category of 'perceived' role to a new unlabelled category of listener/helper, and from this neutral standpoint, help the troubled person to relate *to themselves* the different aspects of truth. The successful outcome of our counselling interaction depends on how well we succeed in facilitating this confrontation of reality.

Even some of our best attempts to build an atmosphere of acceptance and positive regard, within which this exploration can safely take place, can go wrong if we do not try to establish contact with the other person's point of reference. Recognising and acknowledging the position from which the client is speaking enables us to preserve the delicate web of dignity surrounding others. This is all too easy to destroy, perhaps by hurrying to express inaccurate understanding, or by consulting only our own criteria. For example, a helper may call an elderly woman by her first name in an attempt to provide a friendly and familiarising gesture in strange surroundings, but being accustomed to older ways she may see this as a final blow to her dignity.

We can also become too enthusiastic about our counselling work, too ready to see possible clients in every street, in every face. At times we listen *too* closely to social chatter, looking uselessly for meaning where no meaning is intended. At meetings where it is necessary to put forward a suggestion, we can hesitate to make ourselves heard or appear to force our opinions on other people. If we are asked for information, that is all that is required of us. If someone asks us how to get to Cork, they are asking for directions and not a debate about whether or not it is a good idea to go. (Of course if we are accustomed to hearing beyond the spoken words, we may identify an underlying level of distress which could call for a different response, offering the opportunity to discuss the question further.)

EMPOWERING CLIENTS

The use of counselling skills in a helping situation can empower our clients with coping skills for the future rather than providing them with a permanent crutch. For a while, people in distress may need a great deal of support, but to go on supporting them beyond what is essential could undermine their independence.

By suggesting options and offering choices we are giving a client the power to be responsible for herself, and to recognise that she is the only constant in this changing world. These elements of choice and change can be frightening to many people, suggesting that they jettison their protective 'oughts' and 'shoulds' and their carefully learned rules and regulations, learning instead to ask 'why?', and from the answers to forge their own set of values and standards by which to live. We need to remain aware of the threat this apparently chaotic change could be for some of our clients, for while adaptability can be learned, it is a process that needs both support and reassurance.

The counsellor helps the client stand back from his difficulty, to look at it in different ways and from different viewpoints. Why do I act this way, why do I react to other people the way I do, why do I feel anger in certain situations? The answers will lead to a greater self-knowledge, and by looking at this information and learning how to process it, we will have empowered our clients to deal more effectively with future problems, aware of alternatives and choices.

COUNSELLING IN IRELAND

The general acceptance of counselling/psychotherapy as an integral part of our mental health service places an obligation on the representative professional bodies to continue to reach towards higher professional standards and occupational opportunities. Several such professional organisations incorporate counsellors in their representation. I will only focus on the one to which I belong – the Irish Association for Counselling and Psychotherapy (IACP). Founded in 1981, the IACP has an accreditation system for individual counsellors, strict guidelines for recognised training courses, a code of ethics and practice for members (see Appendix), and is continually working to raise the profile and the standards of counselling in Ireland. It has also voted clearly for the future of counselling in co-founding the European Association for Counselling in 1995. Standards and availability of training have increased and improved radically, and the positive effect of this will be the protection of clients from practitioners who offer a service for which they have no formal training or experience, as well as the protection of counsellors themselves from the potentially harmful effects of becoming over-involved with those they are trying to help. Since 1986 the IACP has been in discussion with Government in efforts to achieve the statutory registration of counsellors/psychotherapists. In November 2005, it facilitated an exploratory symposium with a number of interested organisations, and those concerned with counselling/psychotherapy, to expedite this process. It is an exciting and a defining time for the profession in Ireland.

However, Feltham sounds a timely warning when he says, 'I am wary of a professionalising approach that would give all the power to those peddling and measuring atomistic counselling skills and overlook the need for wisdom and social and spiritual sensitivity.'[2] This highlights the delicate balance between formal training and the natural wisdom and common sense of the aspiring counsellor. To suggest that either is sufficient is foolish. It is from their combination that effective counsellors emerge. And in a chapter entitled 'Is Therapy Losing its Humanity?', Mearns and Thorne warn of the dangers inherent in the institutionalisation of a profession, particularly in the helping services where '... they find themselves losing sight of their earlier helping aims and becoming more and more embroiled with the political dimension of their existence.'[3] It calls for a delicate balance between the need for standardising rules and procedures, and the basic imperative that each counselling relationship be unique and open.

These improved standards of training have been matched by increased employment opportunities for counsellors. These include placements in doctors' surgeries; health board categories of counselling work; requests from our law courts for counselling to be made available as part of bail and probation conditions; the expectation of counselling availability following large-scale disasters. The counsellor is very much part of the helping professions today. More and more, voluntary bodies and self-help groups are seeking training for their facilitators and supporters, aware of the large counselling component involved in their work.

And as Irish society changes, so does client profile, and the rate of change has been startling. Counsellors are working with those left behind in the economic boom; with increasing numbers of single parents, struggling to cope with both the demands of a child and with complicated relationship patterns concerning the other parent; with those who are finding the courage to report abuse, sexual and physical, and look for help. Other changes in our society which are being reflected in counselling centres are the introduction of divorce as an option, placing new stresses on relationships; the altered perceptions of institutions, Church and State, creating new dimensions of uncertainty, and the ongoing abuse of drugs and alcohol.

Increasing immigration introduces problems of language and word meanings, where phrases familiar to an Irish population mystify other groups and vice versa. Translators are employed in some centres, creating a new element in a relationship which is already difficult to forge. This diversity of language, lifestyle and culture introduces an element of 'cross-cultural counselling', and yet perhaps counsellors are already more familiar with this concept than they might think. Each individual client springs from his own unique background and family, and the counsellor is accustomed to accepting such differences, despite which she can recognise the underlying similarity of the pain and the problems they bring.

Feltham says that 'The ultimate concern of the counsellor is the promotion of mental health and the critique and elimination of all that diminishes mental and social health.'[4] Trying to help those who are failing to cope with these modern stresses places the counsellor in a pivotal position of awareness of societal needs and pressures.

FUTURE OF COUNSELLING
Different times bring different needs, and today the need appears to be for help in coping with stress, with feelings of lack of

identification, with choice in the face of myriad career options, with a search for stability when the old values are shaken. When advice or example was sufficient, then this was available from family or friends; now that coping or supportive skills are needed, it would appear that these can be learned more effectively from professionals. Paul Halmos described counsellors as 'the moral-cultural *élite* [with] far-reaching influence on the ideological trends of our time...', and further suggested that 'the influence of this professional group is far greater than their numbers'.[5]

Counselling, therefore, is seen as being important today and in the process of becoming more important tomorrow. Bill Law suggests that counselling is a new social movement, coming as the logical result of the developing trends in our society, and creating its own demands for structures and personnel.[6] This new set of ideas forms a link between (or a common element in) the different helping professions. It highlights a larger picture of influence than many counsellors might be aware of, or might be willing to admit, for it postulates very great input by counsellors into the social welfare of the future, and an accompanying responsibility for social change.

Social and economic turmoil creates in people a need and a desire for stability, and they often seek this stability through counselling. Perhaps counselling is giving back to people a feeling of being in charge, of being in control, of being empowered to make their own choices and decisions, and a sense of identity, of being unique, of mattering. Carl Rogers stated the case for counselling and counsellors most eloquently, as far back as 1958:

> If we are thoughtfully trying to understand our tasks as
> ... counsellors, therapists, then we are working on the
> problem which will determine the future of this planet.
> For it is not upon the physical sciences that the future
> will depend. It is upon us who are trying to understand
> and deal with the interactions between human beings –
> who are trying to create helping relationships.[7]

NOTES
1. Richard Nelson-Jones, *Personal Responsibility Counselling and Therapy: an Integrative Approach* (London: Harper & Row, 1984), p. 6.
2. Colin Feltham, *What is Counselling?* (London: Sage, 1995), p. 162.
3. Dave Mearns and Brian Thorne, *Person-Centred Therapy Today* (London: Sage, 2000), p. 41.
4. Colin Feltham, op.cit. (London: Sage, 1995), p. 166.
5. Paul Halmos, *The Faith of the Counsellors* (London: Constable, 1981 edition), p. 48.
6. Bill Law, 'The Concept of Counselling (2)' in T.D.Vaughan (ed.) *Concepts of Counselling*, (London: Bedford Square Press, 1975), p. 80.
7. Carl R. Rogers, 'Characteristics of a Helping Relationship' in *Journal of Personnel Guidance*, Vol. 37 (1958), pp. 6–16.

2. Definitions of Counselling

The fact that the concept of counselling is more acceptable today does not necessarily mean that it is any easier to state accurately and exactly what counselling is. Definitions of counselling range from being too exclusive to being over-inclusive, from attempting to confine it within a narrow, specialist meaning, to trying to stretch the concept to cover every shade of meaning or possible application. Perhaps counselling can be seen as *one* way of helping people. There are others: we can give advice and information, we can attempt to change the environment which is causing the difficulty, we can try to cheer the person up or we can offer practical assistance. If we think it more appropriate, we can offer them counselling. Rogers sums up for me what I am trying to achieve in my work:

> Therapy is not a matter of doing something to the individual ... It is instead a matter of freeing him for normal growth and development, of removing obstacles so that he can again move forward.[1]

In his book *What is Counselling?*, Colin Feltham offers many definitions, ranging from a quotation from Chaucer to a lengthy and most comprehensive definition from the *Dictionary of Counselling*, which begins:

> Counselling is ... a principled relationship characterised by the application of one or more psychological theories and a recognised set of communication skills ...[2]

23

From the point of view of the client, Feltham suggests that it is 'a relationship which is experienced as healing', and he is quite definite that '... it is markedly different from friendship or psychiatry'.[3]

COUNSELLING AND PSYCHOTHERAPY

A common difficulty is the apparently interchangeable use of the words 'counselling' and 'psychotherapy' by some writers, and the determined distinction drawn by others. These distinctions range from the degree of disturbance in the client, to the setting, length of process, type of problem, techniques used, and even the type and duration of the counsellor/therapist's training. Worden, writing on bereavement, suggested *counselling* for normal grief reactions, and *therapy* for abnormal reactions, seeming to regard therapy as a more medical term, for more serious or deep-rooted difficulties.[4] To further complicate the issue, Nelson-Jones suggests that counselling can be seen as 'catering to the needs of the less disturbed', but goes on '... no really valid distinctions can be drawn between the activities of counselling and psychotherapy'.[5] Feltham, in a chapter entitled 'Counselling's Cousins', addresses in depth (and with humour) some of the possible differences between counselling and psychotherapy, and states categorically: 'Apart from differences in jargon and style, with their implicit underlying beliefs, I detect no essential difference between the work of counsellors and psychotherapists.'[6] It would appear that the perceived or claimed differences are between counsellors and psychotherapists rather than between counselling and psychotherapy. 'I believe that many of the professed differences between counselling and psychotherapy stem from purely historical and ideological factors and prejudices ...'[7] It is interesting to note that the current 'label' of the theories of Carl Rogers is that of the Person-Centred Approach (PCA), avoiding the words counselling, therapy or psychotherapy altogether.

The trend today is increasingly towards stressing the shared aspects or commonalities between counselling and psychotherapy, rather than focusing on perceived differences. Patterson also states that 'efforts to distinguish counselling and psychotherapy have not been successful or convincing ... Many authors, beginning with Carl Rogers, use the terms counselling and psychotherapy interchangeably'.[8] Perhaps it is possible to distinguish an element of impatience with the semantics of this debate when Patterson further suggests that professionally trained counsellors or psychotherapists do not try to make distinctions about whether they are engaged in counselling or psychotherapy: they '... take the client where he is and continue with him as far as he can or is willing to go'.[9]

STYLE OF COUNSELLING

If the purpose of counselling is change, then the means by which this is achieved depends on the model chosen by the counsellor, and on his or her personal philosophy: '... counselling theory, which is applied in the give-and-take between and among persons, must be integrated with the counsellor's personal philosophy.'[10] It is not enough to proceed hopefully. Some model or structure is required from the counsellor, so that information provided by the client does not merely pile up. The client is unlikely to have a format, and probably hopes vaguely that life will improve through the counselling experience. And yet the counsellor is not *doing* something to the client. He is facilitating her by providing an opportunity for her to explore and clarify her options, make choices from a well-informed basis, and to take responsibility for those choices. The form of counselling may be decided by the setting within which it takes place, or the presenting problem, whether it be addiction counselling, group counselling, guidance counselling, etc.

A counsellor's unique 'style' will be based on the *theory* of counselling he chooses through reading and study, and on an *awareness* of his values, personal strengths and weaknesses, and method of communication with others. The theory will correspond to his ideas of why people think and behave as they do, and his self-awareness will be achieved through ongoing training and group work. From both of these he will construct or evolve a style of counselling unique to himself.

I believe it is the *realness* of the therapist in the relationship which is the most important element. It is when the therapist is natural and spontaneous that he seems to be most effective ... Thus our sharply different therapists achieve good results in quite different ways. For one, an impatient, no-nonsense, let's-put-the-cards-on-the-table approach is most effective, because in such an approach he is most openly being himself. For another it may be a much more gentle, and more obviously warm approach, because this is the way *this* therapist is.[11]

Each helper, therefore, has to discover the approach or style which is best suited to him, remaining aware that it may not be possible to say that any single approach or interaction is right or wrong, or that the outcome would have been better if dealt with in a different way. Counselling takes place in a once-off unique moment of time, and so many different elements constitute the interchange between the client and counsellor that if any aspect of it did not succeed in its aim, we cannot reproduce the exact moment to see if another approach would have had different results. Yet we need to reflect continually on the outcomes, remaining aware, as Truax and Carkhuff point out, that therapy can be effective, ineffective, and at times, even harmful.[12] Masson goes even further by claiming 'Psychotherapy ... by its nature, is harmful',[13] although his arguments in support of this statement appear to jump from the idea that if something has the potential for harm, then it is harmful. This 'for better or for worse' aspect of counselling needs to be constantly before the counsellor, who is focusing on the needs of the client.

THEORIES OF COUNSELLING

Counsellors need ... knowledge of particular theories of counselling. These theories can provide new perspectives on clients' problems and suggest different ways for counsellors to help. In practice, most counsellors use ideas from several different theories according to how they assess clients' needs at the time.[14]

Counselling theory and practice can be divided, *for the purpose of discussion*, into three main areas: psychoanalytical, behavioural and cognitive. The theories associated with each are based on the way in which the theorist looks at human personality, because in order to institute or encourage change, it is necessary to have some idea as to why people think, feel and behave as they do.

Psychoanalysis is concerned with how *past* conflicts influence present behaviour.

Behavioural therapy focuses on the *problem* behaviour itself.

Cognitive approaches aim at understanding *current* problems and modes of interacting.

Obviously, only a very brief outline of the different areas is possible here, and further reading is needed for a fuller appreciation of the similarities and differences between the various approaches.

Psychoanalytic approach
In accordance with the theories of Freud, this approach is based on the belief that our behaviour is governed to a large extent by our unconscious needs and conflicts, and by the interaction of three mental agencies:

Id: constantly striving for the satisfaction of the basic instincts, the life/sexual instinct and the death/aggressive instinct.

Super-ego: representing parental and moral influence.

Ego: the executive agency, which is trying to satisfy the id, using the reality principle.

The ego is trying to find a balance between the id, the super-ego, and the external world, and the resulting conflict between these three can cause anxiety. If this anxiety becomes excessive, one way of dealing with it is to repress it out of awareness and into the unconscious. Freud emphasised the importance of early childhood experiences, and the different stages of sexual development, when the ego of the child develops defence mechanisms to combat strong sexual impulses from the id.

The aim of psychoanalysis is to strengthen the ego by lifting childhood repressions, and allowing acts of judgement to be made from the ego's present strength. By bringing repressed material from the unconscious up to the conscious level, the analyst helps the patient reassess old conflicts and bring them under conscious control. This is done by the use of (a) *free association*, saying whatever comes into one's mind without editing; (b) *interpreting dreams* in the belief that they form a link with the unconscious; (c) *transference*, analysing the patient's emotional responses to the analyst.

It has been suggested that Freud's theories are based on his observation of emotionally disturbed people, and may not apply to a healthy personality, and also that his emphasis on the sexual instinct as a determinant of human motivation was formulated during the Victorian period of strict sexual standards. However, his acknowledgement of the important role of unconscious conflicts and childhood developments on the human personality has had very great impact on other theories of what motivates people's behaviour. Some later psychoanalysts or *neo-Freudians* place equal emphasis on social influences and on instincts as personality determinants, and are generally more optimistic about the ability of the person to change his behaviour.

Behaviour therapy (or behaviour modification)
The assumption behind behaviour therapy is that maladaptive behaviour is *learned*, and that knowledge about learning techniques can be used to modify or change that behaviour. While self-knowledge and insight into why we behave in a certain way may be worthwhile, they do not ensure behaviour change.

The principles of learning theory include classical conditioning from the work of Pavlov and Watson, and operant conditioning pioneered by Skinner. *Classical conditioning* occurs when a response to a stimulus can be learned through repeated presentation of the stimulus, to the point where the response becomes automatic, and therefore learned behaviour. *Operant conditioning* takes place when the action of a person 'operates' on the environment to produce a reinforcement or reward, thereby increasing the likelihood of the action being repeated.

In order to change maladaptive behaviour, therefore, some form of 'unlearning' is necessary. Classical conditioning techniques are used widely in the treatment of neuroses, alcoholism, etc. Severe anxiety or phobia can be lessened by teaching new behaviour, perhaps by pairing a relaxation response with an anxiety-provoking situation until the relaxation becomes the automatic response, or by pairing the intake of alcohol with a nausea-provoking drug until the avoidance response to nausea becomes the automatic response to alcohol. Likewise, assertiveness training links a new assertive response to the stimulus of interpersonal exchanges, which had previously elicited anxiety and avoidance. This assertive response then becomes associated with the stimulus.

Using the principles of operant conditioning, a therapist may try to minimise factors that are reinforcing or rewarding behaviour which a client sees as undesirable, and to reinforce new and more appropriate behaviour.

Cognitive theory
Cognitive approaches are based on a humanistic theory of the person, emphasising both his ability to bring much of his behaviour under conscious control, and his freedom of choice. Recognition is given to the individual's perception of himself, his interactions with other people and with the environment, and to the belief that if we can change how people conceptualise their world, then their feelings and actions will change too.

1. *Cognitive-Behavioural Therapy* This therapeutic approach combines elements of both behavioural and cognitive therapies, and focuses particularly on how an individual *interprets* life events rather than on the events themselves. Such focus explores how the client thinks about a crisis, the underlying meaning an event has for the client, and how this is affecting their reaction and emotional response.

Becoming aware of this response, in all its negativity and fear, enables a client to identify new ways of dealing more effectively and positively with the crisis. Cognitive-behavioural therapy is seen as particularly effective in crisis situations, where a brief, solution-focused approach is desirable.

2. *Client-Centred Counselling* Also called the Person-Centred Approach (PCA), client-centred counselling is based on the work of Carl Rogers, who believed that the human person is essentially constructive rather than destructive, and if obstacles to growth did not exist, would move towards fulfilling their potential. He also held that human beings can become aware of their difficulties, and have both the capacity and the tendency to move towards psychological equilibrium. Furthermore, he held 'that the human being is basically a trustworthy organism capable of self-understanding and ... of making constructive choices and of acting on these choices'.[15] The counsellor is therefore seen as facilitator, helping the client to identify and define his real needs, and then supporting and encouraging him to attain and fulfil these.

The therapy is called client-centred or person-centred because it is the client who interprets and explains his current attitudes and behaviours, helped by the therapist who neither passes judgement nor criticises, but seeks to clarify the issues. It is non-directive because not only does the therapist avoid giving advice, but the direction of the interview remains in the hands of the client. The emphasis throughout is on helping the person to help himself by finding and using his own strengths, in order to cope more effectively with his life, by making appropriate decisions and taking relevant action. Convinced that her client has the ability to take charge of himself, and that he is capable of taking this responsibility, the counsellor then creates an atmosphere where her client may also come to this realisation.

Some other familiar cognitive approaches are:

3. *Rational-Emotive Therapy* (RET) Assuming that cognitive change will produce emotional change, RET aims at getting rid of 'irrational' ideas, such as 'it is essential to be admired and loved by

everyone all the time', 'people have little control over their sorrow and unhappiness'.

The therapist confronts and contradicts the person's ideas to persuade him to take a more 'rational' view of the situation. Rational thinking is equated with happiness and competence.

4. *Transactional Analysis* (TA) The aim here is to help people become aware of the intent behind their communications, and to help them see their behaviour for what it really is, eliminating deceit and subterfuge.

Therapy takes place mainly in group settings, and communications between group members are analysed in terms of the parts of the personality that are speaking, and the intent of the message. The parts of the personality – Parent, Adult, Child (P, A, C) – are somewhat similar to Freud's super-ego, ego, id.

'Games' (destructive social interactions) and 'scripts' (learned social statements) are exposed for what they are.

5. *Reality Therapy* Here the assumption is that the basic need of all human beings is the need for identity: to love, to be loved, to feel worthwhile. Denial of reality leads to irresponsible behaviour, which results in loneliness and pain. The therapist helps the client clarify his values, evaluate current behaviour, and decide on a realistic plan of future action, having examined the consequences of such future action.

It must be emphasised again that this section gives only a bare outline of the major theories, and that there are many more approaches to counselling theory and practice than are mentioned here. Clear and concise outlines are available from many sources, including Nelson-Jones,[16] Patterson,[17] Boyne,[18] Feltham.[19]

For the purpose of explanation, the dividing lines have been stated here more bluntly than they may occur in practice. Furthermore, many counsellors today 'find themselves dealing flexibly, and therefore eclectically, with their clients; the same procedure does not fit all clients …'[20] and the variety of combinations is endless.

Feltham also suggests: '... it is difficult to see how counsellors can be wholly satisfied with any narrow school of therapy, when the very diversity and complexity of human beings surely challenges the possibility of ever arriving at a comprehensive theory of what human beings are psychologically ...'.[21] Fusing different theories and adopting different components can be seen as a development in the study of human behaviour, an attempt to look at the whole person rather than a piecemeal study. Depending on the individual therapist, the combination of theories and therapies will be a reflection of her attempts to find a 'best-fit' for her client and his problems, utilising also compassion, wisdom, and other characteristics of her personal style. Constantly striving to recognise the needs of the client effectively, and to offer appropriate help, the counsellor who finds a single theoretical base too narrow and too confining adopts an eclectic approach, selecting what will be most effective for this particular client at this particular time.

However, I do believe that it is essential that counsellors work from a fundamental base of theoretical knowledge and self-awareness. The person-centred approach is a 'state of being', from which the counsellor tries to be unwavering in her acceptance, empathy and genuineness towards her client. No matter what form the work takes, these attributes remain the bedrock on which the counselling relationship rests. Eclecticism must never be merely a rag-bag of counselling skills, when the counsellor is hoping for the best and waiting for inspiration: it springs from creativity and from the risk-taking which is part of the work of counselling, as well as from our underlying philosophy of human behaviour and our steadfast belief in the process of counselling.

NOTES

1. Kirschenbaum, H. and Henderson, V. Land (eds) *The Carl Rogers Reader* (London: Constable, 1990), p. 379.
2. Colin Feltham, *What is Counselling?* (London: Sage, 1995), p. 8.
3. Ibid., p. 9.
4. J. William Worden, *Grief Counselling and Grief Therapy* (London: Tavistock Publications, 1983), p. 35.
5. Richard Nelson-Jones, *Practical Counselling Skills* (Eastbourne: Holt, Rinehart and Winston, 1983), p. 1.
6. Feltham, op.cit., p. 46.
7. Ibid., p. 42.
8. C.H. Patterson, *Relationship Counseling and Psychotherapy* (New York: Harper & Row, 1974), p. 6.
9. Ibid., p. 6.
10. Angelo V. Boy and Gerald J. Pine, 'Counselling: Fundamentals of Theoretical Renewal' in *Counseling and Values*, Vol. 27, No. 4 (July 1983), p. 254.
11. Germain Lietaer, 'Authenticity, Congruence and Transparency' in David Brazier (ed.) *Beyond Carl Rogers* (London: Constable, 1993), pp. 21–2.
12. Charles B. Truax and Robert R. Carkhuff, *Towards Effective Counseling and Psychotherapy: Training and Practice* (Chicago: Aldine Publishing Co., 1967), p. 5.
13. Jeffrey Masson, *Against Therapy* (London: Fontana, 1990), p. 299.
14. E.A. Munro, R.J. Manthei and J.J. Small, *Counselling, A Skills Approach* (New Zealand: Methuen, 1983), p. 15.
15. Richard Nelson-Jones, *Personal Responsibility Counselling and Therapy: An Integrative Approach* (London: Harper & Row, 1984), p. 14.
16. Ibid.
17. C.H. Patterson, *Theories of Counseling and Psychotherapy* (New York: Harper & Row, 1980).
18. Edward Boyne (ed.) *Psychotherapy in Ireland* (Dublin: Columba Press, 1993).
19. Feltham, op. cit.
20. Ibid., p. 89.
21. Ibid., p. 89.

3. Necessary Elements in Counselling

ATTRIBUTES

Examination of the counselling process of necessity focuses on the counsellor. The client is the variable, unique in each counselling encounter. The counsellor is the constant, and her expertise lies within herself, in her personality, in her training, and in the skills she has acquired. Examining the process, therefore, is made easier by looking firstly at the personal characteristics of the counsellor, and secondly at her learned skills. This arbitrary distinction is not intended to be either exclusive or all-encompassing, and it is important to remain aware that these attributes and skills both shade into each other, and constantly complement each other.

Attributes here are seen as the characteristic qualities of each person, which can be enhanced or diminished by experience and by increased self-awareness. Skills are examined as practised abilities, capable of being studied and learned. Both the skills and the attributes are necessary, for it is in their combination that expertise and effective counselling are achieved. Yet Patterson warned that 'It is not the behaviours that lead to effective therapy but the effective therapist who tends to behave in certain ways …'.[1] If we accept that there are many forms of effective counselling, perhaps it follows that there are many different combinations of personal characteristics shown by people who function successfully in this area.

In 1958 Carl Rogers identified and isolated the characteristics of congruence or genuineness, empathic understanding, and unconditional positive regard as the specific ingredients in the counselling process which resulted in successful outcomes. These

34

factors had previously been recognised and emphasised, but Rogers suggested that they were not only necessary components for good counselling, but also that they were sufficient in themselves to bring about desired change.

In 1967 Truax and Carkhuff brought these necessary elements beyond the confines of Rogerian theory. Reviewing the available research evidence, they concluded:

> Despite the bewildering array of divergent theories ... several common threads weave their way through almost every major theory of psychotherapy and counselling, including the psychoanalytic, the client-centred, the behavioristic and many of the most eclectic and derivative theories.[2]

These threads they identified as accurate empathy, non-possessive warmth, and genuineness, basically identical to those outlined by Rogers. (However, while acknowledging their debt to Rogers, they considered that these necessary ingredients, growing 'out of Freud's historic development of the "talking cure"',[3] were not in themselves sufficient for effective counselling.)

Difficult to identify, and even more difficult to quantify, the degree to which these core qualities are present in counselling and therapy appears to be a major determinant in the successful outcome of counselling; this is true regardless of the model or style being followed, or of the setting or type of problem. They underpin the therapeutic relationship.

> Of the myriad theories of counselling and psychotherapy, no research has proved that one theory is more effective at helping all clients, though it seems generally agreed that being able to set up a working relationship by communicating the core qualities of empathy, acceptance and genuineness are essential underpinnings for any counselling ...[4]

However, the form this working relationship takes, and how it is engendered, can differ from theory to theory.

Accurate empathy

Empathic understanding or accurate empathy is one of the most misunderstood terms in counselling. Empathy is trying to understand what the client is feeling, from the client's frame of reference. It is not what the counsellor might feel in similar circumstances, because the perception of events is obviously different. It is not sympathy, because while being sorry for another's difficulties is part of being human, this does not demand understanding.

Empathy (or accurately understanding the feelings of a client) does not mean sharing those feelings, but in Roger's words, it is 'to sense the client's private world as if it were your own, but without ever losing the 'as if' quality …'.[5] In order to be effective, empathy must be conveyed to the client, who needs to be aware that this accurate understanding is being experienced by the counsellor. Failure to convey this understanding could leave the client still in a state of isolation, perhaps feeling rejected by a counsellor who neither cares nor understands. For example, an honours student who expresses anxiety and fear before an exam could be told, in an attempt at reassurance, that she is certain to pass, that she will feel better in the morning, that it's just 'nerves'. In effect, this leaves her alone with her fears. However, even if we had never experienced a similar exam anxiety, we can recognise her fear and convey our recognition to her. We enter into and are conscious of *her* anxiety, not our own nor our perception of its causes.

In addition, this effective empathic response may go beyond the client's current perspective to a possible hidden frame of reference. This, if accurate, could reflect a deeper, hidden response of the client to a given situation.

Unconditional positive regard

Also described as non-possessive warmth, this regard need not be voiced, but it is essential that it be conveyed to the client. It incorporates a regard for the client's worth and value as a person, a concern for his welfare, and a respect for his humanity. It is perhaps the nearest we come to loving another person in the truest sense of wishing him well.

The form our expression of this non-possessive warmth takes, whether sharing a silence or not expressing criticism, depends on our acceptance of our client at any given moment. This regard will be non-possessive if we take care not to burden our clients with expectations they have to live up to, so that the person we are trying to help retreats from us. Objectivity and detachment are required, because if we become too emotionally involved, our perspective narrows to theirs. Neither should our client ever feel that her failures cause us personal disappointment, because this could add a further burden of guilt to someone who is seeking help and feeling inadequate.

This positive warmth needs to be unconditional if our client is to feel safe to explore and examine her difficulties. We need to accept, unreservedly, what our client is, not what we would like her to be, nor what we think she ought to be. Our love and our regard must never be conditional on what she says or does. Childhood experience of conditional love and affection is often a basic cause of the relationship problems which bring people to counsellors. 'Be a good girl, and Mammy will love you', and if the child behaves badly, mother withdraws her love, sometimes even to the extent of locking herself in her room, or by leaving the house, and threatening not to come back. Not only is love withdrawn, but the mother's physical presence also, and as the whole family is punished because one child offended or disobeyed rules, guilt may be added to the fear. Through repetition of similar parental responses, the child learns one simple rule at an early age: 'I will be loved when I am good, and *only* when I am good.' Years later, the adult may be still striving to placate and earn the regard of those important to her, using love as a weapon against those who love her, or as a currency to buy and maintain control. The therapist who fails to show unconditional positive warmth may merely reinforce the habits of relating to others which are causing problems; a counsellor who maintains the unconditional nature of her warmth and acceptance could illustrate a role model for future relationships and new standards towards which a client could aim.

Sometimes a client will test the reality of our non-judgemental regard by proposing some outrageous future action. Reassured by our continuing regard, they may then feel safe enough to reveal some past action of which they are ashamed. Unconditional positive regard is part of the ability to differentiate between the criminal and the crime, the wrong and the wrongdoer. Our regard is for the person, irrespective of his actions. Our clients are already focused on their problems and faults, where they have failed or gone wrong. They do not need a counsellor who reaffirms this or who joins them in self-criticism. Instead, we can transmit warmth and acceptance of their human reality, and emphasise their courage in attempting change.

Genuineness

The ability to be genuine, or congruent, to our clients is very much the outcome of the personal development of the counsellor. Understanding our own emotions and being aware of our reactions allows us to concentrate on the feelings of our clients. This self-knowledge enables us to be open and receptive, without any artificial concern about the image we are conveying, and with no need for defensive attitudes.

People in distress are often extra-sensitive, alert to the least possibility of criticism or any break in attention, aware of the finest threads of anxiety or tension in the counsellor. It is essential that the counsellor bring to the counselling relationship both sincerity and honesty, which is what is required of the client who faces sometimes uncomfortable truths about herself and her life and attitudes. Any self-conscious role-playing will hinder the openness and receptivity of the counsellor. (This does not, of course, mean behaving as we wish or as we feel at any time during the session. Yawning because we are tired might be a genuine reaction to a late night, but it may well signify boredom to the client!) Congruence is rather a willingness to be open, to be truly oneself.

Genuineness allows the development of trust between client and counsellor, because it allows us to be ourselves in each session. We do not have to maintain a certain persona over many sessions with a particular client; we do not have to remember how we presented ourselves from one session to another. We are ourselves without packaging or presentation, and as this constancy becomes apparent to our client, she also realises that our positive regard is unchanging, that basically we mean what we say, we are what we seem, and an atmosphere of trust can then grow between us. This attribute of genuineness also facilitates self-sharing, the ability to express our own feelings and ideas when we choose to do so and when the interests of the client require it. Sometimes it can be valuable to admit to failing an exam when the client is agonising over a failure. It lessens the fear that failure is irretrievable. We can give tacit permission to a client to acknowledge a threatening feeling. For example, a client who is very angry with an unreasonably demanding mother may be fearful of admitting her anger because society insists that mothers be loved and cherished. She can be facilitated by the counsellor saying: 'If my mother said/did that to me, I would be very angry with her.' Here the genuine response of the counsellor renders it safe to admit to such feelings, and also presents a precedent of angry feelings with which the client can agree or disagree as she wishes.

However, self-sharing of this nature is not always timely. Sharing the experience of a client who has been assaulted may confirm that you believe her story, that you still accept her, and that you will face the future with her, but it might be quite inappropriate to show your own anger when your client is still at a fearful and ashamed stage. Similarly, if a wife were to describe harsh treatment from her husband, we might be tempted to express pity for her and anger towards her husband. But if she is feeling sadness, love and fear, then our pity and anger might be quite out of place.

Self-awareness

Awareness of these basic attributes of non-possessive warmth and regard for people, accurate empathy, and genuineness can be achieved by concentrating on our own growth. This awareness is essential in order to enhance the degree to which they are present in us as counsellors, to increase our knowledge of their application, and to ensure that they are conveyed accurately to our clients.

Gerard Egan outlines a portrait of the helper or counsellor:

> Ideally, they are first of all committed to their own growth – physical, intellectual, social-emotional, and spiritual – for they realize that helping often involves modeling the behaviour they hope others will achieve.[6]

We ourselves are the constant in all counselling relationships. The clients, the situations, and the problems are the variables. So it makes practical sense to concentrate training on the constant element, in order to increase our understanding of ourselves. In Russia, where psychotherapists receive four years' training, the first three of these are devoted to self-knowledge and self-awareness.[7] The underlying philosophy would appear to be that skills and competence in different areas and knowledge of different schools of counselling are not as vitally important as the growth and maturity of the person who will exercise them.

Self-awareness allows us to know our own strengths and weaknesses, to be aware of how far our training and maturity will sustain us, and to know when our client needs assistance outside of our capacity. It enables us to be at ease within ourselves and within the counselling relationship, because if we are unsure of our ability, uncertain of our competence, then our hesitation will be transmitted to those we are trying to help.

ADDITIONAL CHARACTERISTICS

Imagination and creativity, enriched by experience and study, can be of great help to the counsellor. This is true not only when a client is reliving a situation unfamiliar to the therapist, but also when a client is trying to plan future action, and the counsellor wishes to offer new perspectives on available alternatives.

A sense of humour is valuable, in the counsellor as well as in the client, and we need to respond to any attempt to lighten an atmosphere of tears and depression. This needs to be treated cautiously, however, as heavy-handed or inappropriate attempts at humour could quickly destroy a growing relationship. Perhaps equally important is the ability to smile at one's own mistakes, and not to take either oneself or one's counselling role too seriously.

Simplicity and the avoidance of jargon make it easier to establish trust with a nervous client. It is very tempting at times to use a technical phrase when we feel insecure ourselves, but if a sharing, trusting atmosphere is growing, its fragility may not withstand the sudden introduction of a textbook term which implies superior knowledge. A client describing bizarre behaviour may not be helped by having that behaviour described as 'obsessional', or a 'manifestation of some defence mechanism', or even as 'bizarre', whereas the ordinary response of 'you feel you just have to check all the locks again and again before you can go to bed' acknowledges the behaviour, conveys understanding, and invites exploration of the reasons or the feelings behind the actions.

Patience is also a necessary attribute in the counsellor. The pace of a counselling interview is often in the hands of the client; any attempt to hurry or move ahead may be regarded as pressure, and firmly resisted. It is important that the client is aware of the time that is available for the interview, be it ten minutes or an hour, and it is often the client who will decide how to fill that time, whether to plunge ahead with some revelation, or wait until another day. This waiting can stretch from one session to another and to yet another, as the client circles some topic, gathering the courage to face and share some buried traumatic event or memory. We must be patient if we are going to give him the space necessary to make that decision.

These are merely a few of the other desirable qualities of the effective counsellor. They can be enhanced and nourished without ever expecting to achieve perfection in them. And obviously these are also qualities which will enrich any relationships we have, not just those of a counselling nature. As Rogers says:

> It is not stated that psychotherapy is a special kind of relationship, different in kind from all others which occur in everyday life. It will be evident instead that for brief moments, at least, many good friendships fulfil the six conditions. Usually this is only momentarily, however, and then empathy falters, the positive regard becomes conditional, or the congruence of the 'therapist' friend becomes overlaid by some degree of façade or defensiveness. Thus the therapeutic relationship is seen as a heightening of the constructive qualities which often exist in part in other relationships, and an extension through time of qualities which in other relationships tend at best to be momentary.[8]

Very often, we recognise these positive attributes most clearly on the occasions when we fail to exercise them. We can be very pleased with a certain interview, and equally disappointed with our counselling the following day. It is important to know about these attributes, to be aware both of their significance, and of the need to become more proficient in their use. Then we can grow in our understanding, both of our clients and of ourselves, and as counsellors seek always to change for the better. Counselling is about change, for both clients and counsellors.

NOTES

1. C.H. Patterson, *Theories of Counseling and Psychotherapy* (New York: Harper & Row, 1980), p. 667.
2. Charles B. Truax and Robert R. Carkhuff, *Towards Effective Counseling and Psychotherapy: Training and Practice* (Chicago: Aldine Publishing Co., 1967), p. 25.
3. Ibid., p. 25.
4. Francesca Inskipp, *Skills Training for Counselling* (London: Cassell, 1996), p. 6.
5. Carl R. Rogers, 'The Necessary and Sufficient Conditions of Therapeutic Personality Change' in *Journal of Consulting Psychology*, Vol. 21 (1957), p. 99.
6. Gerard Egan, *The Skilled Helper* (California: Brooks/Cole Publishing Company, 2nd edition, 1982), pp. 26–7.
7. Information gathered by the author during a personal interview with a therapist of the Bechterov Institute, Leningrad, 1985.
8. Carl R. Rogers, op. cit., p. 101.

4. Skills

The word 'skill' might be considered to be too measured and technical for the relationship evolving in counselling. Its strict sense is 'practised ability' (*Concise Oxford Dictionary*), and it is in this sense that it is used here. It is sometimes suggested that counselling is effective solely because of the human relationship that is formed by an emotional climate of love and acceptance. Alternatively, the notion of skills can be brought to extremes of importance, the counsellor being seen as someone with technical expertise and training, applying these techniques when and where she thinks best. However, these two approaches can be combined, the skills being interwoven with the attributes necessary for a good counselling relationship.

> These skills of good human relating involve both self-awareness and technique, with neither being sufficient on its own. Here self-awareness and a caring attitude to clients are sharpened by a more disciplined approach to treatment and responding decisions.[1]

This blending of skills and attributes with 'neither being sufficient on its own' is very far from the notion that counselling skills can be learned and applied at will. Skills are not merely techniques for problem-solving or measurement, which the counsellor carries around in a mental tool-bag, selecting and sharpening for different clients. Rather, the combination of attributes and skills in the counsellor results in an approach which uses caring skills, and seeks to create a relationship within which change and growth can safely occur.

These skills are in constant use throughout the counselling relationship, binding together all the differing facets of the counselling process. Establishing a relationship, responding to our clients, encouraging change – none is possible without the underlying practice of these skills. Outlined here are some of the basic requirements on which the following chapters are based.

COMMUNICATION

Examining the intricacies of accurate and effective communication makes us aware of the many difficulties of understanding what others are saying and meaning, and of being understood by them.

The process of pinning a concept down to a rational thought, constraining that thought into a verbal strait-jacket, transmitting it clearly to someone who may or may not be listening intently, who then has to translate it against his own mental background: this is like trying to guess at the picture of a jigsaw puzzle with half the pieces missing. Little wonder that in general conversation, even with close friends, we often get it very wrong. Indeed, the real wonder is that we ever manage to get it right!

The forging and maintaining of all kinds of relationships is based on effective communication, and the counselling relationship is no exception.

Attentiveness

It is necessary for the counsellor to be entirely focused on the client, in order to be fully attentive to all the words and signals combining to bring us the client's message. This form of total concentration on another person is not commonplace, and it demands that we learn to empty ourselves of our present concerns during the time when we are fully present for this client. This ability to leave our own baggage aside, to forget tiredness and domestic preoccupations, can be practised and learned by the training counsellor, so that eventually we can enter the relationship space as fully as our client. If we were to find ourselves in a session where we were unable to divest ourselves of everyday concerns, perhaps during a time of particular stress for ourselves, then it might be wise to explain this to our client, and make an appointment for a later date. If we are unable to be fully attentive to this client, the addition of her stress to our own might injure us both.

Eye contact

It is not sufficient to focus attention on the words and thoughts of the client. It is vital that this attention is conveyed to her, and maintaining eye contact is the most effective way of indicating our interest. Even in an ordinary conversation, it is disconcerting to look at someone and find them gazing out the window. If the person we are speaking to is wearing sunglasses, we somehow feel she is hiding her real self and may be oblivious to what we are saying.

Maintaining eye contact is like a light shining towards another person, rather than a beam focused on them. We are looking at the client, not watching her, and this visual concentration means that our attention is obvious whenever the client looks towards us. Clients who have difficulty with eye contact themselves, using fleeting glances to check if our attention is still present, find reassurance in discovering over and over again that we are still with them, still attentive.

Where eye contact is not possible, such as in telephone counselling or if the counsellor or client is not sighted, then the task of the counsellor is made more difficult, but the client need not feel unacknowledged. One of the dimensions of a good helping relationship may not be present, but it is not being avoided or neglected. On a radio programme, a traveller spoke of what hurt her most in her dealings with the settled community. It was not doors shut unheedingly, nor the refusal to give food or money, but the failure to make eye contact, when people did not look directly at her. She then felt unreal, without substance, her very existence denied. As 'mirrors of the soul', our eyes may reflect our thinking, but are also seen by others as reflecting our attention.

Non-verbal communication

If we listen merely to the words spoken, although we recognise themes and interpret underlying feelings, we will miss an important source of information being given by the client about his difficulties. This is body language, or 'body-speak' – a range of signals which convey information about our mental state. Often we are not alert to these, either in ourselves or in others. We are less able to disguise these physical signals, and often they belie the verbal messages we are sending. In theory we are aware of many of these signs, and we speak of a 'poker face' as the deliberate attempt to conceal emotion. However, in practice the more obvious are impossible to hide, such as becoming red in the face with anger, or pale from shock, but the lesser signs of tension or distress, such as clenched hands or rapid eye movements, are often beneath our awareness. For the counsellor, these lesser signals call for our attention, and we learn to add our awareness of these to the accumulating verbal information, like carefully reading the small print on an important document. Posture, nervous movements, inability to relax, inappropriate laughter or smiles, all these can indicate the emotional state of our clients more accurately than spoken words. When a client who is usually impeccably dressed, with hair carefully groomed, the picture of neatness and tidiness, comes to the counsellor with a generally unkempt appearance, it indicates some change in her approach to life, whether she is ready to admit it or not. Her physical state proves that all is not well with her.

The counsellor who is attentive to these non-verbal messages will be aware that he himself is conveying similar physical information to the client. When there is accord between the verbal and the non-verbal communication, they merge and blend into a single transmission. It is when there is contradiction that the physical message becomes more visible, and it may convey the truer message, because it is more difficult to disguise and less immediate to our conscious control.

Silences

Perhaps one of the hardest parts of listening, in the counselling setting, is dealing with silences. In our everyday conversations silences rarely occur, and when they do, they are often causes of embarrassment. We hurry to fill the gap, we search frantically for some phrase or topic to restart the conversational engine which has stalled, we even have phrases such as 'angels passing' or 'someone walking on my grave' to cloak the quiet moment, to drown the silence. In the counselling setting silences can be seen in a different light as they can be most productive if handled correctly.

When a client pauses to think or to consider what she has just said, it is easy to hurry in with an interpretation (often wrong) or a reassurance (often misplaced). This eagerness to express our understanding is frequently unjustified, because if the client is finding her way towards understanding a feeling or an idea she has expressed, it is unlikely that we will be so quickly before her in accurate understanding. If a client says thoughtfully, 'Perhaps I react too harshly', often the words linger for her consideration, and may be followed by, 'No, that's not it' or, 'Yes. I never thought of it that way before'. Either reaction would be positive progress, which would not take place if we were to affirm or deny her spoken thought too rapidly.

BEYOND THE SPOKEN WORD

The client's recording of events or reactions is the main clue we have about the situation which is causing difficulty or unhappiness. This recording sets the scene, fills in background, and reflects how the client sees the situation, how he chooses to describe it, and how much he wishes to reveal. It is the privilege of the client to choose how far beneath the words he wishes to go. We may illuminate areas he has left dark, but the choice of whether to examine these belongs to the client.

Some clients stay with these surface words, merely seeking an audience to nod and smile at the appropriate time. Any suggestion that they go further is evaded, and perhaps a caring listener is all they wish for at this time. This kind of inert listening can be valuable, but it is not counselling, and no real client-counsellor relationship is developing.

Meanings of words

It is easy to forget that different words may have different meanings for two people, not merely in the dictionary sense, but in the learned connotations which a word or concept evokes from experience. A distressed client may speak of going 'home', and we envisage a secure and supportive place for them, while in reality their home may be the source of all the bitterness and misery of conflict. Similarly, our concept of 'mother' may be warm and nurturing, but would have a completely different meaning for a client who is striving for independence. We must listen from the client's point of view or framework. We must try not to sift what the client is saying through our own fine sieve of experience. For example, stories of violence and strife may be creating an excitement or tension on which some people thrive; the use of forceful words may be their normal mode of expression, and not a reflection of inner tension or stress as we would see it.

Repetition of words or phrases

If a counsellor becomes aware that a client is continually repeating a particular word or phrase, it is helpful to look for clarification. Perhaps a client is using a phrase to describe someone else's behaviour, often quite inaccurately. 'Her nerves are at her, all the time. I tell her that too, that her nerves are at her, but she won't listen to me and she's fighting all the time with the kids. I'm getting out if she won't do something about them.' Here the husband just wanted his wife to get some help from her doctor, but she was convinced that he wanted her locked up because he thought she was 'mad'. Asking him to explain what he meant by 'her nerves are at her' was sufficient to clear up their misunderstanding.

Repetition of a word can result from a client being preoccupied with some image or state of mind, and being quite oblivious of this. 'You've used the word *bizarre* several times since you came in, and I'm not quite sure what you mean by it', invites clarification.

Recurring themes

A further aspect of this is remaining alert for recurring themes, trying to sense the structures of the client's problem or distress through the confusion of words and emotions. These themes can offer a clue to an underlying aspect of the trouble, one which perhaps the client hasn't considered or even imagined. For example, describing her marital difficulties and her feelings of uselessness at home, a client was convinced that she was suffering from 'endogenous depression', a label she had latched on to and brandished as a direct ticket to medicine and instant cure.

However, continual reference to her age indicated that her depressive feelings were related directly to her fears about growing older, and she needed support in coming to terms with this, rather than medication. Fearful of her fortieth birthday, she had failed to make the connection between her age and her despondency, and yet in the course of the work, the recurrent theme of age and advancing years was the clue for the therapist.

UNDERLYING FEELINGS

Looking and listening can become concentrated on the thinking and actions of the client, as expressed in words and body language, to the exclusion of his feelings. Discussing this possibility, Murgatroyd says: '... all forms of helping are concerned with thinking, behaviour and feelings since these three features of the person are inextricably linked.'[2] He suggests that there are times when it is not only desirable, but essential, to concentrate on the emotions of clients, as for example when a person tries to discriminate between different thought-blocking feelings or tries to understand new and powerful emotions no longer under his control.

It is often painful to look beneath the surface of the defences which we have built around ourselves as a division between our public and our private selves. The transparent honesty of a child, expressed in sudden statements and undisguised expressions, is soon veiled by the repetition of phrases like: 'You mustn't get angry with Granny', 'Never say that again', 'Big boys don't cry'. Some kind of reticence is necessary for living, but our defences can become impregnable, even to ourselves. To look then for the reasons for actions, or the causes for relationship difficulties, and to explore their emotional content, may not only be difficult, but also painful and emotionally threatening. Seeking to divert from the aching sadness a client is experiencing may be because WE cannot tolerate staying with this level of pain. The counsellor must learn not to minimise the pain or the threat, however unimportant the cause may appear to be. If emotional stress and worry can cause headaches and stomach ulceration, their psychological impact can be equally severe.

It is understandable therefore that a client often seeks to intellectualise his feelings, or to place the cause for them outside himself: 'This climate depresses me', or 'The people in my office really drive me mad'. Helping a client to pinpoint the driving emotion behind his actions is often at the centre of our counselling role. A man struggling with feelings of guilt about the way he treats his mother, about the fact that he only has time to visit her once a week and when he does they usually quarrel, may need to examine *why* he cannot be kinder and more attentive to her. On the other hand, he may need to examine an underlying anger towards her, which he is afraid to admit (because everyone must love their mother) and which he might instantly deny if it were abruptly suggested. Part of the counselling skill of responding will offer the idea of anger for consideration in such a way that it can be looked at as a possibility.

LISTENING TO OURSELVES
Beneath our awareness of our clients runs the need to listen to ourselves, to be aware of our own body language, our own responses, our own words. The counsellor needs to be alert to the filters that can exist between herself and her client, clouding the growing relationship between them – cultural filters about people who speak in a certain way, prejudicial filters about certain actions, etc. Egan adds a further possibility, where a counsellor has studied abnormal human behaviour as part of her training:

> Unless you are careful, psychopathology filters can play too strong a role in your listening – that is, you can begin to interpret too much of what you hear as abnormal human behaviour. What you have learned

> may help you to organize what you hear, but it may also
> distort your listening.[3]

He suggests, however, that recognition of these kinds of filters is the first step in counteracting them.

As counsellors, we can be over-tired, distracted, or preoccupied with our own worries at times, and unless we are consciously aware of the possibility that these will affect our attitudes, they can influence our interactions with others. We can also be over-eager, too conscious of our own responses, and unaware of the more subtle aspects of the growing relationship; we need to find a balance between being aware of our own responses, yet concentrated on those of our clients.

DETACHMENT

Despite its connotations of uninvolvement and remaining aloof, detachment in the counselling sense does not mean regarding tears with a dispassionate eye and waiting for the client to stop weeping. It is rather the ability to go with our client into his anger or despair, without bringing our own intense feelings with us. This enables us to achieve two objectives.

Firstly, we can retain the focus on our client, exploring his emotional reactions from his perspective, without the complication of having to explore our feelings too. For example, if an angry client shouts blame at us, identifying us with the world he feels has wronged him, how will it help if we too get angry? We will have ceased to look at his hurt and anger, and will instead be partly focused on our own. We will no longer be sitting with that client. We will merely be sitting opposite him.

When a client touches some depth of feeling within us, we need to be able to place that feeling to one side, not repressing it but postponing our expression or examination of it. Thus we are free to stay with our clients while they experience their emotions, and to be present with them when they wish to explore the reasons which triggered their reactions. Far from being uninvolved, we suffer with them, but we suffer *their* pain and grief, and not our own. We are there to support them while they experience their feelings, and we afford them the personal space to try to come to terms with them.

Secondly, detachment enables us not to become emotionally over-involved with our clients. Identifying too closely with their lives can cause us to lose our objectivity, joining them in their single perspective rather than being able to illuminate other alternatives for them. Over-involvement can also place an intolerable burden on our clients, who may find themselves trying to cope with our feelings as well as their own.

It is very important, both for our own well-being and for that of our clients, that we are constantly aware of our limitations and our emotional boundaries, and that we have interests and relationships outside our counselling work.

CLIENT SKILLS

In any counselling or helping interaction, there is the possibility of the client learning problem-solving or coping skills, whether or not the counsellor intends to teach these. Egan describes these 'client skills' as:

> physical, intellectual, and social competencies that are necessary for effective living in the areas of learning, self-management, involvement with others, and participation in groups, communities, and organisations.[4]

The counsellor helps clients to 'muster their resources' in order to cope with problems of living. The implication is that each client has the resources within himself and merely needs help to discover and effectively employ these. If this is so, once discovered, they are there for future use. By encouraging someone to stand back and review their present situation, by helping them to recognise choices and alternatives in their lives, we are creating for them a model of coping and surviving their present crisis, which they can reapply in future difficulties.

All these skills and applications of listening may appear to be more than any one person could hold in her mind at one time, but through practice, they become part of the whole counselling process, fitting together in our professional capacity. We make the skills of counselling part of us, second nature in our responses, so that we are free to focus on the individual we are trying to help. It is reassuring to listen to the voices of experienced counsellors, such as Tyler:

> One of the rewards of continuing counselling experience is the realisation that what one says need not be fluent or elegantly phrased in order to be effective.[5]

It is also useful to remember that our work as counsellors may facilitate the movement of the other person from stage to stage, but the entire process is characterised by the courage and honesty of the client.

NOTES

1. Richard Nelson-Jones, *Practical Counselling Skills* (Eastbourne: Holt, Rinehart and Winston, 1983), p. 16.
2. Stephen Murgatroyd, *Counselling and Helping* (London: British Psychological Society and Methuen, 1985), p. 83.
3. Gerard Egan, *The Skilled Helper* (California: Brooks/Cole Publishing Company, 2nd edition, 1982), p. 73.
4. Ibid., p. 11.
5. Leona E. Tyler, *The Work of the Counselor* (New Jersey: Appleton-Century-Crofts, 1983), p. 41.

5. Establishing the Relationship

The practical aspects of counselling are very personal to the individual counsellor, since they depend on her method, style, clientele, place of work, etc. Because of this, statements or examples from someone else's casebook might not be directly relevant, but may have their value in contrast, or even in contradiction. It is not possible to say, 'This is the right way, or the right thing to do, and no other will suffice', given the variety and scope of human responses, both of client and of counsellor. It is possible, however, to see where a response is inappropriate, or where another reply might have been equally appropriate, and a method of counselling to suit the individual's style can be modified by reading suggestions and ideas from other sources. Morse Code has an exact alphabet of dots and dashes, but it is possible for the expert to recognise the style and characteristics of individual operators. In the same way counselling techniques may be learned, but their application is always twinned with the personal style of the counsellor.

The initial stages of counselling are the most important, since both the continuation and the final outcome of our counselling efforts depend on how we handle these. Our attitude towards a client begins even before we meet, and it is important not to establish a picture of the person or the problem in advance. No matter how many unhappy married couples we see, no two of them have the same difficulties or perceptions of their relationship, and yet it is so easy to begin a session with a fixed image. 'Perhaps you could see Mrs Murphy', says a colleague. 'A difficult lady, intent on a separation.' Despite ourselves, we form a picture which is later hard to dislodge.

At the beginning of a client-counsellor relationship we cannot be aware of the whole picture. After all, we do not have any information about facts, feelings or circumstances. It is by being attentive to our client that we will be introduced gradually to this person's life, and it is essential to remember that there is a larger picture. It is like putting together the edge pieces in a jigsaw puzzle: we are establishing a frame, taking the easiest pieces first, and not knowing at the beginning whether we will see the finished work. To try to guess at details in advance will merely lead to confusion later on. As counsellors, when we meet a new client we have two initial aims. Firstly, we are hoping to establish a relationship, and, secondly, by encouraging our client to explore, we hope to begin to clarify the need which has brought her to us.

Practical aspects

Obviously the setting in which we see clients will vary according to the nature of our work. It may be in a clinical context, in a corridor, in our homes or offices, in a prison. Whatever the surroundings, there are some basic requirements, a few of which are discussed here.

(a) Privacy It is essential that a client feel free to express thoughts and feelings privately. Some people can speak freely of themselves before others, but allowances need to be made for those who cannot. Often those who appear most voluble and open are the ones who require a private setting before they can discuss what lies beneath the surface of their words. The creation of this private space ensures that a person is aware of the counsellor's full attention, able to be themselves, and to speak without fear of being overheard or interrupted. The level of noise off-stage, as it were, does not appear to be as important as the need to create an oasis within that noise. A setting within earshot of a noisy school playground, or the echoing of construction work, can be quite adequate as long as a cocoon can be created within which both counsellor and client feel secure. Neither thunder nor wind, cars nor planes can disturb the peace thus created.

(b) Comfort It is difficult to concentrate on our troubles if our feet hurt or if we are shivering with cold. Adequate heating, comfortable chairs, sufficient space in which to be at ease – the counsellor is responsible for the provision of all these. The general setting of the room is also important. Placing a table between client and counsellor can indicate a barrier, a demarcation line between the person in need and the person seen as having all the answers, a visible underlining of a possible 'one down' feeling within the client. The décor should be neutral, neither clamouring for attention nor depressingly dull, and the lighting needs to strike a balance between the dimness of conspiracy and the brightness of interrogation. The heightened sensitivity of the person in distress is very real, and a client may notice something in a counsellor's room that she might not be aware of in a friend's house. If we are accustomed to sitting in a fixed position when we see clients, it is a good idea to test the client's chair and viewpoint from time to time. Their image of the surroundings may be quite different from ours, and perhaps less positive or less encouraging.

(c) Time constraints The importance of being punctual for a pre-arranged session hardly needs to be stressed, and it is a good idea to let a client know in advance how much time is available, whether it is an hour or twenty minutes. Alerting her when only five or ten minutes of a session remain gives her an opportunity to mentally 'pack up', to detach herself from the intensity of a session, and to begin to put on again the public persona which she had left aside during the counselling time. Unless we have a well-developed time sense and can know to the nearest five minutes what time it is, it is essential to have a clock within our vision, possibly behind the client's head so that we can see it without turning aside. Nothing is more disconcerting than speaking to someone who is constantly looking at her watch. An additional clock within the client's view enables her also to be aware of the time that remains, and perhaps then to choose how she would like to spend that time.

(d) Note-taking It is generally agreed that it is not acceptable to make notes during a session. Information such as name, address, phone number, medication, etc., may be noted either at the beginning or the end of a session, but I need to remain concentrated on the person before me. The very act of writing down what a person is saying introduces a new element into the counselling session, and the client may begin to focus on the notes rather than on the free expression of thoughts and feelings. It is as if the act of recording demands more accuracy and neater sentences, and even raises the suspicion that this will be quoted against them later. It also sometimes raises doubts about confidentiality. I find that recording can best be done after a session, since the total listening and intense concentration produce a very accurate recall. Also it is not the names, ages and facts that are important; it is the client's perception of these, and the feeling-tone beneath these statements that matters. These could hardly be recorded in the course of a session. However, some form of record-keeping is important because seeing a number of people during one day can easily result in the last client overshadowing all those before; five minutes spent after a session writing one page of notes, highlighting points to be recalled at the next session, and underlining gaps or emphases noted is of great value when this client comes back again.

Introductions
The first few minutes of meeting a new client are difficult to assess, and yet important in building up the trusting relationship necessary to all counselling. The instinctive likes and dislikes we often formulate when meeting somebody new may be highlighted for the client, who is perhaps feeling helpless, greatly distressed, angry or extremely sensitive to this new situation. Our job as counsellors is to establish ease and the beginning of trust. We need to become aware of the impact we can have on first-time clients. Our desire to illustrate our competence may be seen as intimidation, our concern may be construed as patronising, our efforts to give the client space and freedom to express herself may be interpreted as uncaring. All manner of misunderstandings can flourish in the first ten minutes!

Some practical guidelines can help us cushion this initial stage, although every counsellor will formulate his own style.

(a) Greetings Approaching a person, rather than waiting for them to approach you, is usually seen as a friendly initial gesture. A handshake, eye contact, using the client's name, and repeating your own (which they may have forgotten) can be helpful.

Hello, Mrs O'Neill. I'm Ursula O'Farrell.

The addition of some friendly comment to bridge the movement from door to chair, or from waiting room to office, is a good idea.

I'm glad you've come.
Isn't it nice to see the sun again.
I hope you didn't get too wet.

These kind of weather comments do not require a response, and yet they bridge the potentially awkward moments with familiar reassurance. Comments that call for detailed reply and discussion, such as travel questions and the relative merits and demerits of the local bus service, can result in an unnecessary prolonging of the conversational interchange. In the same way, unless shock or very great distress create a special need, cups of tea and biscuits can prolong the social nature of the occasion, and make it more difficult to move towards an atmosphere where true counselling can take place, which is the actual purpose of the meeting.

(b) How to begin 'I don't know where to begin' or 'I feel silly talking about myself': these are two common introductory statements by people coming for help. Many people genuinely do not know what the real nature of their problem is, or are not familiar with the words needed to describe their unhappiness, and finding a starting-point is difficult. Also, many clients think there is a set formula they should follow: 'Do you want me to describe what happened – do you want me to just talk?' Reassurance is required, and brief statements to the

effect that this time is theirs – 'we have an hour' – that there are no rules, that you are demanding nothing from them. 'Tell me how it is right now', and 'I know it isn't easy' are the kinds of response appropriate at the beginning. Often it is only when we give people space to speak freely and without interruption that they can begin to define what exactly is causing pain, what they wish to change. Vague feelings of anxiety, general unhappiness with life itself, as well as responses to specific difficulties all bring people looking for help. This is a particularly sensitive time in the counselling relationship, when the normal conversational rules are suspended and minimal responses accompanied by open, caring, attentive listening make possible the tentative beginnings of trust. A client who expressed amazement at her ability to speak openly of events in her family which she had previously been afraid to articulate, even to herself, encapsulated the aim of the whole counselling relationship and setting:

Counsellor: You feel you can say these things here, but you
               would be slow to say them at home.
Client: Yes, I feel safe here.

Again, I would emphasise that the exchanges work for me, but in order to be genuine, each counsellor will discover how she would like to proceed.

(c) *Filters* We often see people in terms of their role. (Who are you? I am the guide / doctor / plumber.) We expect from them attitudes and actions consistent with that role. Some clients see counsellors as 'curers', and they come to have something done to them, some unhappiness dissipated, some painful experience amputated. They may be seeking something we do not have to give, some magic solution. They may in fact see us in a filtered way, coloured by their expectations, and as a result their perception of what we say and of what we are offering may be inaccurate. They attribute to us meaning and power in terms of their own need.

Similarly, at times we can be invested with a kind of halo effect within which we can do no wrong. 'You helped my friend. She's like a different person, so I've come to you.' Here the implied message is 'give me some of the same treatment, and I'll be like her'. 'You remind me of my mother' may imply not merely physical resemblance, but all the connotations of security, safety, and protectiveness that this particular mother may have provided. (Or indeed, all the power, guilt, and insecurity that another mother may evoke.) The counsellor may be unconsciously cast in the role of any significant figure in the client's life, from relatives to teachers to bank managers. We cannot be aware of the variations, and we may never actually know that this process is taking place, but we can be aware of the possibility of this filtering or of being seen through rose-coloured spectacles. This will help us to remember that we are merely facilitating the change in our clients, and that the actual changing is being done by the client himself.

(d) Contracting It is easy for a counsellor working in familiar surroundings to a familiar timetable to forget that these are not immediately obvious to a client. It is important to be clear about the length of the sessions and the form your help will take as this information is probably new to the client, as is the experience of being listened to in this way. It is difficult sometimes for a client to grasp that the time available is hers, to be used as she wishes, to talk, or sit in silence or in tears. Towards the end of the first session, she will need to know if the counsellor can help, does he see the difficulties as insurmountable, can he give her hope. It is important to give space for questions, perhaps about the counsellor's qualifications, perhaps to ask if he has ever heard of a similar 'case'. This is the time to outline the format, usually an hour a week; if there is a fee, to mention the amount and whether it is negotiable, payable at each session, etc. It is a good idea to mention a plan to which the client can agree, perhaps a contract to meet six times and then to renegotiate if required, or to end the sessions then if progress is not being made. Outlining an agreement can clarify the situation for the client, whether she is looking for help in a long-term developmental difficulty, or desperate for assistance in a current crisis. There is of course nothing to hold the client to this agreement,

but it gives an awareness that while one or two sessions may not be sufficient to effect change, the relationship will not continue inexorably and for an unspecified time into the future. The duration may be for the counsellor to suggest and advise, but in reality the client decides, which is important in a relationship where she is going to confide and entrust her innermost thoughts and feelings to the counsellor. Being in this kind of control means that she does not feel dictated to or powerless.

MOVING FORWARD

After the initial introductions, the client begins to outline the problem area as she sees it. The counsellor helps this exploration, facilitating the expression of facts and statements, encouraging her to look at the emotions beneath the surface, clarifying and defining painful areas. In later sessions the counsellor will try to focus on the important or relevant points, lest the clients merely talk on and on, with lots of words and feelings, but little else. The counsellor might indicate her awareness of avoidance by the client, without demanding that this be attended to right now, as the choice of direction is ultimately the client's, but it is essential to allow time, as six sessions merely constitute six hours of the client's life span. Inexperienced counsellors sometimes say, 'I don't know where to bring this client or how to proceed ...', forgetting that it is the client who leads and shows the way. The counsellor needs to move delicately in helping the client explore, and attentive listening will be accompanied by responses not only to elicit information and feelings from the client, but also to convey the empathy of the counsellor. It is quite useless to be attentive and empathic if this is not appreciated by the client, and while a large measure of understanding can be conveyed by posture and attentive eye contact, some input may also be necessary.

(a) *Questions* In everyday human exchanges, if we want information we will ask questions. In a counselling situation, if a client is faltering and uneasy, it is tempting to revert to a question-and-answer style. This may result in knowing the exact ages of a client's children, and the nature of her work, but it is unlikely to have highlighted the basic anger she feels, for example, about one of the children. Whether the child in question is Seán or Seamus, whether he is six or sixteen years old, is irrelevant. She is with you to try to deal with her anger, and this is the area to explore.

When a counsellor does need to elicit information, there are different ways of asking questions. Direct questions can be threatening to many people, particularly in the intimate areas they may be discussing, and interrogation may freeze the beginning of a trusting relationship. 'Why are you angry with Seán?' is confronting this mother with her own anger in an abrupt way, using the strong word 'angry' with the demanding word 'why', and often leading to a response like: 'Well ... not really angry.' The direct question also requires this mother to put aside her feelings of anger and focus on the reasons, moving from the feelings which need to be expressed and explored to the intellectual reasoning. She probably has several answers to the question 'Why?' (he is cheeky, he is always late, he doesn't work at school), but she has come for help in looking at the implications of her anger, and the counsellor here has merely brought her back to the questions she can ask, and answer, herself.

An indirect question, using inflection to reflect the question, like 'Angry?' or 'He really gets to you?', is much more useful. Here the word 'angry' is offered with a question mark, softening its impact, rendering it less accusatory, and allowing the mother to agree or disagree, to own or disown this anger. In the second example, the counsellor indicates that she has understood what the mother is saying, and invites her to explore and explain within her own parameters.

Asking open-ended questions, rather than closed questions, is also more likely to move the interview forward. A closed question, which allows the client to reply with either a 'yes' or 'no' answer, is likely to lead only to further questions. 'Do you lose your temper with him often?' is not only very direct, but likely to lead to a simple denial or affirmation. It will have elicited a fact, but little else. Questions beginning with what or why, with who or where, are likely to be very direct questions, and often closed ones too. It is possible to rephrase almost every question as a statement, offered for clarification.

'What do you mean by that?' can become 'I'm not sure what you mean'. 'Why do you want a separation?' rephrased as 'I feel there are other areas we haven't talked about, which may be part of your decision' makes it easier for the young man to explore, at his own pace, the growing realisation that his marriage is threatened. It is a helpful and entertaining exercise to practise transforming any direct question we think of into a statement:

How much did your coat cost?	= I like your coat, I suppose it was expensive.
Why are you in a bad mood?	= I feel you're cross because you've had a difficult day.
Are you still living with your boyfriend?	= I'm not sure where you're living at the moment.

It would be unrealistic to suggest that a counsellor must *never* ask a question. However, it is so natural to ask questions in ordinary conversational exchange that over-emphasis is perhaps needed to avoid the habit. To quote Egan:

> The point here is not questions in and of themselves but how they relate to and promote or hinder the overall helping process.[1]

(b) *Reflecting back and empathy* The idea of reflecting back what another person says or does suggests merely mirroring the words or actions used. It sounds like a passive response but when used in an empathic way, it becomes far more than merely offering a mirror image.

Empathy is trying to understand what the client is feeling, from the client's frame of reference, and conveying empathic understanding to the client, by reflecting back something of what is understood. Having established this awareness, it is as if the counsellor and the client were speaking the same language, using the same set of symbols, and the client feels enabled to examine and explore the problem area, no longer alone.

Egan differentiates between primary and advanced empathy depending on the level at which this understanding takes place and is communicated, but in the initial stages the counsellor would use primary empathy. This is especially useful when encouraging the client to acknowledge the feeling content beneath the descriptive words he uses. Reflecting back is usually most effective when it is tentative, because no matter how well we are listening, and how much in tune with the client's feelings we think we are, it is possible to be quite wrong, and to reflect back inaccurately, or too abruptly. Examples of inappropriate responses are:

Client: (Speaking hesitantly, with his head turned away)
   I'm twenty-six and I don't make friends easily. There's this man I like a lot. He works the same shift. And I'm afraid … you know …

Response: (without accurate empathy)
   You're afraid to tell him. (This has interpreted the hesitation as fear, but has misplaced it.)
   You find it hard to make friends. (Here the counsellor reflects the first sentence, and steers away from the pain that follows.)
   You think you might be a homosexual. (This response is to the point and possibly accurate but it is sudden and sharp enough to frighten the client even more.)

There are several responses which would illustrate empathic reflecting back, such as:

   You're uneasy about the whole situation.
   You're afraid of what you're feeling.
   You like him a lot.

These responses acknowledge the fear, the liking, and the underlying unease about the relationship. They offer space and acceptance to discuss the whole area further.

(c) Staying with the client It is tempting sometimes to think, at an early stage in counselling, that it is already possible to see the whole problem and what should be done about it. Even if the counsellor were right in these assumptions (and it is rarely as simple as this), she must remember that the client may not yet be ready to confront the difficulty and deal with it. The counsellor needs to pace herself to the rhythm and speed of client disclosure and to remember the complexity involved. Attempts to hurry people along will result in interruptions by the counsellor, which may be seen as impatience and will serve only to distract or distress the client. Even in ordinary conversation, interruptions cause people to lose the thread to their thoughts, and irritate them by signifying lack of interest. Yet if a counsellor is over-eager or tense, it is very easy to jump in every time a client pauses for breath.

(d) Clarification for the counsellor In the first interview, there will be a lot of information which is muddled or vague, and the counsellor may be tempted to stop the client every now and then to fill in gaps which are appearing in the recital. It is usually a good idea to restrain this enthusiasm, partly because it can be unwise to interrupt, and also because shortly after a question mark arises in the counsellor's mind, the answer is often supplied. Where the counsellor is more likely to seek clarification is towards the end of a first session, when he is not sure he has heard something correctly, where he thinks he has heard contradictory information, or very often where he has *not* heard something included. For example, Patricia was outlining difficulties within her family, seemingly centring around her mother, with whom she constantly quarrelled. She had spoken of her father, but sometimes in the present and sometimes in the past tense. It was not clear whether he was alive or dead, living at home or elsewhere, and the counsellor considered it important that his place in the picture be clarified. The counsellor might try to do this in several ways, such as:

I'm not sure where your dad fits into the picture.

or

Perhaps you would like to tell me more about your father.

Clarification may also be necessary if the other person is weeping, or very fearful, because the counsellor may not be able to understand what she is saying, or to hear more than a few words at a time. It is important not to keep up a pretence of hearing, because in time it will become obvious that the counsellor has not followed the story. A remark such as, 'I'm sorry, but I'm not hearing you very well' can be quite acceptable, avoiding a more accusatory 'You're speaking too low, you'll have to speak up'.

(e) Silences We tend perhaps to think of silences as negative, as mere gaps in the mutual exchange between people. In counselling, silence is a time for reflection, for re-hearing something that has been said, for experiencing and maybe moving on from an intense feeling, for reassessing strengths in the light of some discovery during the counselling exchange. The counsellor needs to perceive a period of silence as productive rather than threatening, and to curb natural conversational responses in order to give space to the client. 'I feel very miserable' in ordinary conversation requires an acknowledgement, perhaps a reassurance, and a cheerful reply: 'Things can't be that bad' or 'It will look better in the morning'. This in effect may be saying that the listener cannot cope with the misery, is unwilling to share it, and is handing it back to the speaker to deal with herself, or wait until it goes away. The silence used in counselling situations is doing exactly the opposite. It is a tacit acknowledgement of the misery, of its reality and its pain, and is allowing the client time and opportunity to explore it, experience it, and try to see if anything can be done about it. This kind of silence is not just keeping quiet and not speaking. It is more an absence of interruption, respecting the client's need to face up to the misery in the presence of a sympathetic counsellor. It allows the client to hear herself, to hear the echoes of what she has already said, and

sometimes even to reach a further step in clarification and reality as she assesses, in the silence, the statements she is making.

It is important also to remember that some clients, who may previously have experienced lack of response as punitive, may find prolonged silences difficult to cope with, perhaps even threatening. Here it is often sufficient to acknowledge the difficulty: 'I get the sense this is not easy for you.'

(f) Exploring further This is the recognition by the counsellor that it is not sufficient to stay on the surface of the words, or to stay strictly within the client's framework. It is necessary to enter that framework, but as the client's difficulties have been caused by being trapped there, if the counsellor follows suit, there will be no change, no advance. It is the beginning of a search for reality; to find what is *really* troubling this person, what this person is *really* saying. After all, if the real problem were what the client is saying and outlining, then it would probably have been within his power to change it without having recourse to a counsellor. It is precisely because he is caught within the narrow confines of his own perception that he is seeking a wider perspective, and the counsellor will encourage her client to explore beyond these parameters.

To facilitate this exploration the counsellor tentatively offers insights into feelings, linking one half-finished thought to another.

Mary: Peter's been gone a month now, and while I cry a lot, I am also very angry at him. Every time I think about him I could scream with rage, and then I cry. I think I hate him.

The counsellor here could answer, 'You're very unhappy', and at an early stage this might be an appropriate response, helping Mary to further explore this misery. But if this statement had been made after she had spoken a lot about her grief and misery, it would be time to explore a little further, and the counsellor could say:

Perhaps you're angry at him because you love him so much, and this gives him power to hurt you.

or

You feel angry and perhaps you feel helpless too?

This statement offers several new perspectives for Mary to consider, including the idea that she may be avoiding expression of her anger, and trying to cope with her unhappiness through misery and tears alone.

This exploration is a very delicate task, because people have built up defences for themselves, and the counsellor is asking them to dismantle these and look at their reality. For some people their defences may be holding their world together, and they will be very reluctant to step out from behind them. Indeed, some clients look at the prospect of change, decide it is too dangerous, and opt to remain where they are. The present pain is at least familiar, and less threatening than the prospect of change.

Exploration is a time for particular caution on the part of the counsellor. It is very easy to use inappropriate responses, becoming judgemental ('I don't think you should hate him, Mary'), patronising ('That's a very understandable reaction in the circumstances'), interpretative ('I think you really mean that it's all his fault'), or advice-giving ('What you really need is a good holiday'). The task here is to offer glimpses of other possibilities, and allow the client time to consider these, and then to accept or reject them as she thinks appropriate.

FOCUS ON FEELINGS

Creating an atmosphere of trust and attentive listening may encourage a client to talk, but relating anecdotes is not sufficient for change. The gathering of facts and information may have set the scene, but the feeling-tone beneath the words is at least as important. Not many people are in the habit of examining their feelings, least of all with a stranger, and describing a close relationship like marriage can too easily stay at the 'He said to me' stage. One of the main tasks of counselling is to help people look at the feelings which often cause the very actions that they are anxious to change.

(a) *Identification of feelings* Feelings can often merge and mask one another. A mother who sees her child almost run over by a car quickly replaces her fear with anger at the child, and perhaps a good scolding for being so careless. A counsellor may have to counteract this merging of emotions by continually encouraging a client to focus on the feelings underlying what he is saying.

Client: The boss told me I'd have to travel round the country, and I said straight that he couldn't make me.

Counsellor: You didn't want to travel.

Client: I'd be no good at talking to strangers and anyway who does he think he is? I'll get on to the union.

Counsellor: You feel angry at being pushed around.

Client: Well, I suppose he's the boss and he has the right. But I don't want to go.

Counsellor: You feel you'd be unhappy outside Dublin.

Client: Not so much unhappy, but not in charge of what's going on.

Counsellor: Perhaps you feel things will change while you're away?

Client: In fact I'm afraid someone else will get promoted while I'm rushing from place to place.

Finally this client admitted his fear, through the layers of anger and unease, and was then able to discuss whether it was genuine and what to do about it. If we can recognise how much we ourselves contribute to our difficulties, then there is a new possibility for change.

Client: John talks very loudly when he gets annoyed and it always makes me angry when someone shouts at me.

Counsellor: You don't like people shouting at you.

Client: No! I feel they're going to get violent.

Counsellor: And violence makes you angry.

Client: Well, no. Not angry. Actually it terrifies me. I think I've always been afraid of people getting violent.

This is now a new feeling of fear, which appears to underlie the anger for this client. Prolonged discussion of the anger might have been merely discussion of a symptom. Helping the client to explore her fear of violence, its origin, and why it is linked to loud voices, may not lead to an elimination of the fear, but will lead to an understanding of it. And full understanding could bring this client to say to herself:

> John is shouting at me. That makes me afraid, but I know why. I know it is not John that I am afraid of, but the echo of an old fear inside me. So there's no need to get angry with John. I wonder why he's shouting? Does he shout at everyone? Perhaps he's angry and doesn't know why.

(b) Owning our own feelings Reluctance to admit to feelings of fear, sorrow, anger can also be compounded by an inclination to attribute the causes of our feelings to other people and events. If a client says that her children make her very angry, this suggests that change can only occur on the part of the children. If their behaviour could change, then her anger would be unnecessary. The suggestion that the anger is hers, and that one of the triggers which makes her angry is her children's behaviour, gives her an understanding of these feelings, and some insight into how to change. Similarly, a teacher experiencing unhappiness in her school:

> I get on fine with the children, but some of the other teachers really annoy me. I go in every morning ready for anything, but they moan and groan and they make me miserable for the rest of the day. It's getting so bad I dread going in.

She is looking at her feelings of misery as being directly controlled by her colleagues. No matter how contented she is, she believes they have the power to deprive her of happiness. She accepts and carries their burden of complaints all day, feeling helpless.

If she could rephrase 'they make me miserable' to 'I become miserable when they complain', then she is not *made* unhappy, she *becomes* unhappy. This apparently simple change of image from passive object to active subject can make a new exploration of her unhappiness possible. Is it just in the school situation that she is depressed? Does she feel 'different' because she has no cause for complaint? Is she taking ordinary grumbling too seriously? She can focus now on her own unhappiness rather than on the actions of others, which are quite outside her control, and seek to change it.

This need to own our feelings implies self-responsibility, because once our reactions can no longer be attributed to someone or something else and the possibility of change becomes real, then the decision to change or not to change is ours, and nobody else's.

(c) Accepting our feelings It is important to help our clients understand that feelings in themselves are not bad. We all experience anger, grief, joy. It is what we do with our feelings, our expression of them, that can cause difficulties. Repression of feelings can result in pent-up emotional constraint, which can in turn lead to physical illnesses like ulcers, headaches, or to violent uncontrolled outbursts when the repressed feelings become too strong to be contained. A counsellor can give her client permission to express feelings which may appear dangerous to him, for example by offering a statement with which he can agree or disagree:

Counsellor: If my father did that to me, I'd be very angry.

Here the hitherto unacceptable feeling of anger towards one's father has been mentioned and thereby made acceptable by the counsellor. This kind of response is more valuable than the direct question:

Client: My wife drives me mad.
Counsellor: What does she do that makes you angry?
Client: Well, for a start she spends too much money, and she always keeps me waiting when it's time to go out …

This question merely produced a list of events and actions, and kept well away from the actual emotions of anger. Similarly, glossing over the feelings of a client with vague reassuring remarks may at times be a tempting response, but it will not deal with the underlying causes of the trouble.

Client: I'm afraid in the house at night.
Counsellor: There's no need to be afraid. Your family are all in the house.

This client wants to talk about her fears and what to do about them. The counsellor, however, chooses to ignore the reality of the fear and says that it is unnecessary. The client knows this, but she needs help to cope with the reality of her fear.

A short statement acknowledging the emotion, followed by space to expand and discuss it will usually result in the exploration of these feelings and the reasons for them. 'You're frightened of something' or 'Tell me about it' are good responses, encouraging exploration by the client. Sometimes a client speaks of loving someone, and appears unable to express her anger towards the same person, as if love and anger were mutually exclusive. Pointing out that it is possble to love someone AND be angry with them at the same time can come as a revelation. It is of course this exploration of feelings that makes it so important for the counsellor to be at home with her own emotional responses. If we personally have failed to come to terms with the death of someone close to us, then trying to help a client cope with his grief will not only be extremely difficult for us as counsellors, but will probably prevent us from encouraging the client to mourn as he needs to. Also, if we have problems with our own angry responses, then the anger of a client may trigger a rage in ourselves which will profit neither ourselves nor our client. It is essential that the counsellor recognise her own triggers, and is not afraid to remain with the client as he deals with his strong emotional reactions.

Throughout all these aspects of helping the client move forward from the initial position of giving information and talking, it will be obvious that a total respect for the other person and for their present needs and troubles is the underlying thread. What is revealed or outlined at this stage determines the kind of change, its form and progress, which the counselling process will produce. This is the foundation on which the rest of the counselling process builds, and if it is faulty or inaccurate, the results will be unsatisfactory.

NOTE
1. Gerard Egan, *The Skilled Helper* (California: Brooks/Cole Publishing Company, 2nd edition, 1982), p. 102.

6. Counselling as a Process

BEYOND LISTENING

A counsellor may be the best listener in the world, but merely to listen is to be too passive. If we believe that one of the main objectives of counselling is to offer our clients new perspectives and alternatives to a narrow view of their difficulties, then we must be able to order and pattern the information we are receiving. Looking and listening is most vital in the opening stages of a counselling relationship, while the person is quite unknown to us. Later in the relationship, when we become more attuned to the presence and manner of our client, we will become more automatically aware of the nuances of his speech and behaviour, and the need to concentrate on looking and listening will be less acute.

We will have established contact, and will then be able to begin a more active kind of listening, relating what is being said now to what was said during the last session, aware of how a certain feeling is linked to something said some weeks before. In the same way, the client will be at ease in the situation, and more receptive to these indications of patterns and connections.

The client comes to a counsellor at a certain stage: if she leaves the counsellor at the same stage, then the process has not resulted in change. The beginnings of counselling are the start of self-exploration, and the data that emerges can be put together in a different sequence by the counsellor, thus leading to a new frame of reference. It is not sufficient to allow the information to lie inert between counsellor and client once the information-gathering stage is past, because all the information, emotional and factual, spoken and unspoken, will not effect change unless it is sorted, assessed, and absorbed.

> Although the process of understanding what the client
> means is a very complicated, demanding and necessary
> task, it alone is not sufficient.[1]

It is the responsibility of the counsellor to remain constantly aware that there is a larger picture, the picture of the client's life up to now. The client has come because he is seeing, and reflecting to us, only a tiny part of this picture, probably from a single troubled perspective. Remaining *aware* of this larger canvas, which is not visible to us and perhaps not even to our client, makes it easier for the counsellor to tease out the more important facets for the client to focus on. On the basis of the information we have received up to now, we can facilitate exploration rather than try to control or direct our client. The counsellor does not *do* anything to the client. She may assemble the pieces into different patterns, and offer these to the client as alternatives. The client chooses which pattern he prefers, or which seems the most appropriate for him. Then the counsellor can assist the client in planning how best to implement this choice.

> Counsellors not only help them [clients] piece together
> the data produced through the self-exploration process
> but also help them probe wider and look deeper in
> order to find the 'missing pieces' they need to
> understand themselves and their problem situations.[2]

RESPONDING

If we think of counselling as based on change, we see it as a developing and ongoing process. It is not enough to have a vague and hopeful idea of good nature and love resolving all difficulties. We need to be aware of our own style, and also to have some framework within which to work. In our response to clients, we are probably situated somewhere between two extremes. In our efforts to reach detachment, we could withdraw our persona completely, leaving a client feeling ignored or invisible. Alternatively, obvious concentration and too responsive an attitude could either overpower a client, or seem like avid curiosity. We need to strike a balance between attentive interest and regard, and a respect for the possible nervousness and natural reticence of the client.

Having listened carefully and closely, the counsellor will make some response, initially to indicate her understanding of what is being said and explained, and later to help the client move forward from mere recital of facts and feelings. The nature of this response can be looked at under different headings.

> It can also be said that a problem situation well explored, defined, and clarified is well on its way to being managed.[3]

Egan emphasises that behaviour change cannot take place until it is quite clear what needs changing, and one of the main tasks of the counsellor consists of helping the client be more specific about the area of difficulty. Broad statements like 'I'm very unhappy' or 'I'm worried all the time' are too insubstantial to deal with in themselves, and the feeling aspect is too vague. 'He's driving me mad' encompasses so many unanswered questions that clarification is essential, even before exploration. What is meant by the client using this phrase? (It is never wise to assume that your meaning of a term, especially a colloquial term, is the same as that of the client.) Does she really mean that one person is the sole cause of her agitation, or are her circumstances such that he is merely irritating her? Is this the outcome of a long-term relationship that is going through a bad patch, or a last-straw situation where something has irretrievably broken apart?

> When clients talk about themselves, they do so in terms of *experiences* (the things that happen to them), *behaviours* (what they do or fail to do), and *affect* (the feelings and emotions that accompany and relate to experiences and behaviours).[4]

Clarification consists of linking these three components, helping the client see the relationship between them, and, in this clarity, identifying the aspects that need changing. It is helping a client expand from 'I'm very depressed' to 'I'm very depressed since I started a new job last year' to 'I'm very depressed since I started a new job last year where the boss hassles me, and I'm not able to stand up for myself'. This is a problem area outlined and expanded to the point where ideas for changing this situation can now be suggested by the client himself, who may not previously have made the connection between the timing of the depression, the new job, and the pressure from a domineering boss.

Summarising

A client can discuss a problem for a whole session, or even for several sessions, and have reached a stage where she is repeating ideas and feelings. She may in fact be stuck at the recital part of counselling, and it is possible for a counsellor to gather threads together, and to highlight what appears to be the main area of stress. 'We have discussed your difficulties at home for some time now, and you appear to be saying that the main area of conflict concerns your job, and that John is resentful of the time you spend outside the house. Although the money you earn is needed, and you like getting away from housework for a while each day, there are rows in the evenings when you both come home. Perhaps these differences between you could be discussed more easily at the weekend, when you're both less tired.' This summary highlights the job as the immediate conflict area, but has also indicated triggers to anger. By collecting together the salient points, the counsellor is also underlining a possible flashpoint (evening discussion when both are tired), and mentioning the possibility of sidestepping this. Summarising can also be useful at the beginning of sessions, when a client has had time to consider some important aspect raised at the last session, or if he feels he is not progressing, or if he ended that session with plans to do some specific task. For example, if he decided to look at the reasons for repeated arguments at home: 'At the end of our last meeting, you decided to try to discover why there are constant arguments at home. You felt that if you recognised the triggers, you might not feel compelled to join in. Perhaps you'd like to talk about how this went for you.' If this exploration had been rewarding, the client would be disappointed to miss the opportunity to look more closely at it with the counsellor. It could discourage future plans, which might similarly be left hanging in the air, as if they were of no importance or interest to the counsellor.

Offering different perspectives
Sometimes a client is unwittingly looking at his world and his problems from a single perspective, and twist and turn as his mind may, he cannot see other than a single outcome, or a single cause. While he stays looking at the problem from this fixed viewpoint, it may well be impossible to change, whereas examining a situation from several angles may suggest different ways of dealing with it. It is the task of the counsellor to offer these different perspectives. If the client were able to do this, he would probably never have come to the counsellor. Mary, a single mother, anxious to allow her child's father access to his daughter, yet confused by the way it is turning out, offers a good example:

Mary: He rings up when it suits him, and says he'll take Frances for the weekend. He never asks if this is a good time for me or for the child. He just phones, usually on Friday, and says he'll pick her up. And then again, it may go five or six weeks, and we'll hear nothing. But there's nothing I can do.

C.:   You feel it's important that Frances sees her dad, but you would like to know in advance when she's going to visit him.

Mary: Maybe it's unreasonable, but sometimes I'd have arranged a visit somewhere, and then I'd have to cancel it. Because as he says, I have her all the time.

C.:   I'd get angry if I had plans made and had to cancel them in a hurry. Especially if it happened quite often.

Mary: Yes. I get really mad, and then I feel guilty, because it would be worse if he didn't care about her.

C.: It's important for Frances that she see her father, but it's also important for her to have stability and routine in her life. Perhaps her father could let you both know in advance which weekends he will be free to look after her, and then she could look forward to her visits.

Mary: I didn't think of that. I was only thinking that I didn't want to deprive Frances of the chance to see him. I suppose it is unfair to just hop it at her out of the blue.

C.: Perhaps it would be possible to give Frances a choice in the matter, allow her to choose if this or that weekend would be her preference.

Mary: Then I'd be giving him the opportunity, but asking him to plan a little in advance. But how would I tell him? He always make me feel guilty and selfish, and puts down my ideas.

C.: You might find it easier to write him a note about it, and talk about it later.

Here the counsellor has offered several new and different slants on the whole idea of access for this father. Mary had been caught into the single idea of not depriving Frances of time with him, and had found herself unable to see that there were various ways of arranging this. It is important from the non-directive standpoint that the counsellor remains aware of the concept of *offering* or *suggesting* different approaches, and avoids direct advice such as: 'I think you should put a stop to this', or 'Just write a letter and tell him'. These methods may have the same effect of introducing ideas, but they do not allow the aspect of personal choice on Mary's part. She might find herself thinking that a new approach must be right because the counsellor *told* her to do it, or alternatively lack the necessary follow-through because it was not her own choice. At the end of this session, Mary could opt for change:

Mary: I think I'll write and ask him to meet me and talk about it. By writing I'll get a breathing space, and he'll have time to think it over himself.

or

Mary: The next time he rings I'll tell him I'm busy, and to ring
          back next week, that we can't just hop and trot as he
          orders.

or

Mary: That's right. It's not good for Frances to live in uncertainty.
          I'll tell him he can see her once a month.

She might also choose to do nothing, and continue to allow
Frances to visit at her father's whim, rather than have a
confrontation. However, she is now aware that she does have choices,
and feels no longer caught in a trap of someone else's making. Being
able to identify choices brings empowerment.

It is also important for the counsellor to remember that this is the
point Mary came to clarify. Whether she chooses to return for a
further session to deal with her anger and guilt, hinted at in her
description of the situation, is also a matter of her choice.

Identifying patterns
Not only is it important to clarify and summarise for the client, but it
is also the job of the counsellor to identify patterns in what the client
is saying. During the listening time, so many ideas and words and
descriptions are heard, that the storing of information is a
continuous task. Searching for patterns is the result of a type of
'matching', holding two apparently similar ideas together, and
perhaps discarding the connection between them with the addition
of a third fact. For example, a client outlines an episode at work:

John: The boss read me for being slow to respond, and I came
          very near to just getting up and going, leaving the job and
          all. No one speaks to me like that and gets away with it.
C.:   It sounds as if you were very angry indeed.
John: I was fit to kill him. I remember at school when I was
          seventeen a teacher spoke to me like that, and I just walked
          out and never went back. My parents wanted me to do the
          Leaving but I didn't bother.

The counsellor can focus here on the conditions at work, on what the boss said that caused the anger, but it could also be a time of rematching the two episodes, and responding with a statement about the possibility of a pattern becoming visible:

C.:   Something in the boss's voice or tone was the same as in the teacher's?

This kind of connection is best proffered as a tentative statement, with which the client can agree or disagree, because as a direct question it might be heard as an accusation: 'Do you not like being bossed around?' or 'Do you think he has no right to tell you what to do?' Such a question can also be answered by 'yes' or 'no', which leads to another direct question or a change of subject, rather than an opening of thoughtful discussion. Two skills come together in this focusing; the deductive ability to see a pattern or relationship between the two items, and the tentative offering of the insight for further exploration. At times the connection may be dismissed, but returned to later as if it were a connection made for the first time by the client. This gathering of threads and matching of feelings yields new data and new insights and, if put together effectively, a whole new frame of reference is established. This results in a larger picture from which new choices can be made.

CHALLENGING OR CONFRONTATION

> ... *confrontation* means anything that invites a person to examine his or her interpersonal style – emotions, experience, and behaviours – and its consequences (for instance, how it affects others) more carefully.[5]

Here Egan uses the word 'confrontation' together with 'invites', thus showing that he is not suggesting anything abrupt or harsh when he speaks of confrontation. If the idea of confrontation is seen as an attack or too strong a challenge, then it will not succeed in its aim of understanding more fully some form of behaviour or interpretation of events with a view to changing these. Challenging can be effective in many different cases, some of which are outlined here.

1. A client may have a completely different image of herself and of her behaviour from that held by others, in this instance the counsellor. For example, she will say, and believe, that she is incapable of being clever or original in conversation, and that people will think she is ignorant or laugh at her. As a result she is unable to meet other people with any ease, and her social life is very constricted. Challenging her is essential for her progress, and it may be done effectively within the context of the counselling interview:

    > You say you cannot be original or fluent when you speak to other people, but you are very well able to express your ideas and feelings to me in these sessions.

    The response here is likely to be: 'But this is different. I feel safe here and I know you are not going to criticise me', leading directly to a new tack: 'Then your difficulty is not with the actual expression of ideas, but with the people to whom you are expressing them.' This may not sound like a significant change, but if the client had spent time exploring whether or not she was intelligent, when her real problem was perhaps a fear of being criticised or despised by others, it would have been time spent chasing the wrong idea. By challenging her belief that the difficulty is within herself, and suggesting instead that it is in her relations with others, she comes to see that a solution lies in practising social skills rather than learning, or trying to learn, to be constantly entertaining.

2. It may be useful to challenge a statement made repeatedly by a client such as: 'That's the way I am', or 'Of course I can't change the way I'm made'. No matter how undesirable the actions or reactions being described are, this kind of statement removes all responsibility, and automatically relieves the client of any need to examine the problem situation. A client describing difficulties

with her adult children absolves herself of all blame, and perpetuates the conflict, when she says, 'But that's the way it's always been in our family, and there's no point in trying to change us now'. The counsellor can respond with a mild challenge:

> But you've come to talk it over, so perhaps you hope that some aspects can change.

or

> And yet coming here is a new departure for you, and that in itself is change.

This highlighting of an aspect of behaviour not acknowledged by the client, or not recognised by her, can move her from categorical statements like 'that's the way it's always been' to seeing that other possibilities exist, and that she does have a choice.

3. Often a counsellor is aware of a marked difference between the words a client is using, and the underlying feeling or meaning indicated by unspoken body language.

Peter: Of course I am used to interviews by now. I've been to many, and usually I get the job I go for, so they can throw any questions they like at me, and it won't bother me; (as he discusses the next interview, he sits tensely, unrelaxed, and shifts several time in his chair).

C.:   And yet I sense you are anxious about this next one. Perhaps this new job/promotion is particularly important to you.

Here the counsellor tries to highlight the nervous movements of Peter by linking them to possible anxiety. (The tentative manner of the counsellor here takes account of the possibility that Peter may be merely uncomfortable in his chair!) By picking up the unease and reflecting it back together with one possible cause, the counsellor opens the way for Peter to discuss some difficult aspects of this future meeting, or equally gives him an opening to bring in some quite different matter which is causing the anxiety. Very often the presenting topic (in this case the interview) may be merely used as an introduction to open proceedings. Job interviews are a safe topic when compared with, for example, marriage difficulties, which proved to be the underlying reason here for his anxiety.

Peter: Yes, I am very uneasy, and it's not about the job. It's about my marriage. Things are not good between us. I find it very hard to find the words ...

In this instance, if the counsellor had stayed with the spoken words, and not recognised and challenged the unspoken anxiety, the session might have continued with a discussion of the interview prospects, and the sought-for opportunity to discuss marital difficulties might never have arisen.

4. It is often productive to challenge the way a client constantly blames others for her emotions or her reactions to situations.

Joan: I sometimes think my sister-in-law does it on purpose. It's four months now since Jack died, and she goes on and on about him, what he was like when they were small, things he said. She really depresses me and I don't think I'll ever get over it at this rate. She lives with us, and when the children are in, it's worse, because they join in. She's making me so miserable; do you think I should ask her to move out?

Here Joan had not yet dealt with the grief and misery caused by the death of her husband, and appeared to believe that her present unhappiness was caused by her sister-in-law. As long as she persisted in this belief, there was no visible reason for her to look inwards to her unhappiness, because she could 'blame' someone else. Owning our own feelings, accepting that they are part of us, rather than caused by some outside person or agency, allows us to recognise and deal directly with our anger or unhappiness, and we feel less helpless. Listening to Joan, the counsellor thought that she was afraid to consider her unhappiness because it was too overwhelming, and instead was translating her misery into anger towards her sister-in-law, whom she had cast in the role of 'someone who makes me sad'. As long as she considered her sister-in-law responsible, then Joan was helpless and unable to do anything positive about her grief, because it was being caused by someone outside herself. Here the counsellor challenged her view of the situation.

C.: Remembering makes you miserable, and you feel that if you were on your own, you'd try to forget. Perhaps you feel other people speak too casually about Jack? You must miss him a lot.

Here the counsellor reflects what the client had said, challenges the basic idea that the unhappiness is solely caused by others, and invites Mary to speak of her grief openly.

Phrases such as 'He made me angry', 'People in the office really annoy me', 'Parties bore me to tears', all place the cause of the emotional reaction firmly on someone or something else, and thereby eliminate any need on the part of the speaker to do anything about it. They claim to be powerless because they were made to feel something. If we can encourage a client to change these statements to: 'I am very angry because of what he did', 'I get very annoyed by people in the office', 'I get bored at parties', the rephrasing places the responsibility for the feeling firmly on the client's shoulders. 'He made me angry' begs the question 'Why?', and leads to a discussion of someone else's behaviour. 'I am angry because of what he did' leads to discussion of why this behaviour triggered her anger, what it was inside herself that responded with anger to some action. If this can be identified, then there are choices – perhaps to avoid this person rather than get angry; to examine her own feelings and see if she can change, and if so, whether she wishes to; to recognise the trigger to anger, and by anticipating it, lessen its impact; to recognise the trigger and choose to react with anger each time.

By challenging the language used, the counsellor also challenges the thinking process behind it, and restores to the client the power of making choices, and of being in charge of herself.

5. It is useful to challenge a phrase or a word by clients if they appear to have borrowed it from some other source and to be using it as an explanation for their own difficulties, without fully understanding or assessing its meaning. To take shelter behind a jargon phrase or a childhood description, as an interpretation of an action or emotional response, may be merely substituting one difficulty for another, and removing the need for action.

A client who suffered from intermittent but severe depression constantly appeared to console herself by repeating: 'Depression is anxiety-linked', as if this statement in0 itself should lessen her depression. When the counsellor queried what exactly this phrase meant to the client, she was not fully sure, but by searching for meaning, she found other insights which were helpful to her. If the counsellor had accepted the phrase as a real insight, rather than a phrase borrowed from elsewhere, then counsellor and client might have been working on different levels of meaning and cause for some time.

To use a further example, Peter was a young man experiencing difficulty in asserting his independence within his home setting. He spoke consistently of 'respect', due in different measures to parents, teachers, clergy. It became apparent to the counsellor that he was using the word 'respect' as if it were in direct conflict with the idea of 'independence', and eventually she challenged:

> I'm not sure what you mean by respect. Perhaps we could talk
> a little about this.

Peter spoke further about respect, defining it as having equal meaning to 'subservience', and thus causing him to feel guilty each time he tried to be independent in any way. As he struggled with word meanings, he came to see that 'being respectful towards' someone was quite different from being 'subservient', and eventually he began to become more independent, without feeling 'disrespectful'!

These are different ways a counsellor can use the skill of challenging or confronting to help her clients move towards new perspectives and insights. It is again important to stress that the counsellor is not doing something to the client, and is not making judgemental comment on what the client has said. Rather, the counsellor could be said to be using the information shared by the client, rearranging it, and re-presenting it in a different light or a different shape for the client's consideration. Where an atmosphere of trust and confidence exists, this skill can be very effective in indicating where changes can be pursued. However, if challenging is used too soon in a counselling relationship, it may not only be inaccurate, but may be misinterpreted by the client. In order to ensure that our confronting is neither blunt nor intrusive, we will remain conscious of the need to challenge with a caring and careful approach, always mindful of the good of the client rather than reflecting annoyance, curiosity, or impatience on the part of the counsellor. In this way, even if it is inaccurate or mis-timed, the strength of the relationship and the perception by the client of the counsellor's good intentions will usually minimise any ill-effects. However, challenging must be used with caution, and always with love.

MAKING DECISIONS FOR CHANGE

If the counselling process stays at the informational and anecdotal stages, then it could go on indefinitely. The action and planning time may follow quite naturally after the client outlines her difficulties, or it may arise from the counsellor's highlighting of alternative courses of action or differing perspectives. With some exceptions, such as addiction or crisis counselling, suggesting alternatives rather than issuing directives has two advantages. (A person locked into phobic behaviour might benefit more from direct methods of dealing with the phobia at first. Later when the stress of the phobia is lessening, counselling may be more effective.) Firstly, it opens up for the client the idea of possibilities: 'This is not hopeless, there are some things I could do, I do have some choices.' Secondly, suggesting alternatives leaves room for acceptance or rejection of an idea. However, if these suggestions are offered too early in the counselling process, they may not even be heard, much less accepted as plausible courses of action. They are more likely to follow on from the initial stages with the 'deeper understanding' of which Egan speaks.[6] The balance between not being directive and being merely passive is a fine one, best achieved through Egan's 'responding with understanding'.

> Responding with understanding is perhaps the most useful yet least used response in interpersonal communication.[7]

This movement from thinking to feeling to action is not a series of activities in orderly sequence, but a combined consideration of all three. The idea of change and goal-setting can involve a change of attitude, a change in the way of thinking about a situation, a physiological difference leading to a lessening of stress or anxiety, to increased feelings of contentment. For example, practising deep relaxation techniques can alter sleep patterns and lessen unnecessary worrying. Understanding why a colleague is constantly angry, and realising that the anger is not focused directly at me, can change my attitude towards the angry person. Accepting that an exam failure will not herald catastrophe can help a client think about it in less threatening terms. Whether the client is seeking change in developmental, crisis, or solution terms, identification of the area needing change is the first step. Next the client must actually want to change, and finally a decision must be made about how to change. Hopson put the varied options succinctly:

> Given any issue or problem a person always has four possible strategies to deal with it:

- change the situation;
- change oneself to adapt to the situation;
- exit from it;
- develop ways of living with it.[8]

There is, however, a lot of effort and work to be done between seeing how things might be for the better, and actually achieving the change.

If it were merely a question of identifying where change was needed, and if implementation of that change automatically followed, then the work of the counsellor would end here. There would be no need for counsellors if a troubled person could say: 'I am unhappy. Why? Because I don't like my work. Why? Because the boss treats me unfairly. Then I will change jobs.' And she did, and lived happily ever after!

This idea of change and specific goals is, of course, rarely so tidy in our lives. There are times when a simple decision needs to be made, but usually we are faced with complexities within ourselves and conflicting influences from without. Changes and decisions may range from changing jobs, to redefining our requirements from work, to examining our attitudes towards others. In counselling, these choices will be made by the client, and when the client is choosing courses of action, several points are important to bear in mind:

1. The counsellor has helped to identify areas where change could produce some desired effect, but it is essential that the client make the actual choice of action and acknowledge responsibility for it. Sometimes a client will request direction from a counsellor: 'Do you think if would be a good idea if I ...?' or 'Maybe I should ...'. The client could decide on a course of action to please the counsellor, or because it is what 'mother' thinks is best. These decisions would not be owned by the client and if the action becomes difficult, or he fails to follow through, then he may say: 'It wasn't my choice anyway', 'It's all the counsellor's fault.' It is important that the client acknowledges responsibility for the choice of action.

2. Plans for change need to be specific, and clearly stated. For example, 'I'd love to go to college and do a degree' is wishful thinking rather than a plan of action. The counsellor can help his client to be more specific: 'I'd love to go to college, but I need the Leaving Cert. One of these days I must find out more about doing it.' The stated goal has become the Leaving Certificate first, but it can only be adapted to a practical programme by introducing a time-scale: 'One of these days' needs to be replaced by 'tomorrow' or 'next Wednesday'. Outlining a series of steps from finding out about the entrance examination, to choosing subjects, to allocating time for study, enables this client to think seriously about her aspirations, to cope with the size of her ambition, and to recognise the ongoing achievement of each stage successfully completed.

3. The set goals need to be realistic, and capable of attainment by the client. Helping a client plan a budget when her overspending is causing friction and becoming a threat to her marriage can be a very practical form of help, but unless her aims are within the bounds of possibility, taking into consideration both her needs and her habits, then the chances of success will not be high. Frustration is the only result of formulating goals which are beyond the attainment of the client.

4. It is important that the set goals are not at variance with the values of the client. If a man who is having trouble at work decides, in order to keep the peace, to go along with work practices which run contrary to his own chosen values, then the ensuing conflict within him causes even greater stress than before.

5. In developmental counselling, or when helping someone cope with changed circumstances, the goals are not so specific, yet the same guidelines can be kept in mind. Stated aims can sometimes form a kind of contract between client and counsellor, but if this is too rigid then failure to fulfil the requirements may become a cause for guilt or remorse. As a result, the counselling originally

designed to help becomes instead a cause of new anxiety. Evaluation at a later stage may lead to changing the original plans, in the light of new understanding.

The personal responsibility of the client is highlighted here because even if the goals focused on in counselling meet the requirements listed above, it is the client who will follow through by acting on them. However, having helped someone to discover and choose difficult goals, it is the responsibility of the counsellor to support, encourage, and assist her in working towards these goals. The results of counselling and the success of plans may be to some extent due to the hours we spend with a client, but they are also brought about by her intervening work and thought, and the way she interprets change between sessions. How often our clients surprise us, perhaps by having taken a step we would not have thought within their capacity. Change is never static, and the process is not only between client and counsellor, but also between the clients and their living surroundings.

NOTES

1. Susan K. Gilmore, *The Counselor-in-Training* (New Jersey: Prentice Hall, Inc., 1973), Century Psychology Series, p. 253.
2. Gerard Egan, *The Skilled Helper* (California: Brooks/Cole Publishing Company, 2nd edition, 1982), p. 155.
3. Ibid., p. 84.
4. Ibid., p. 71.
5. Gerard Egan, *You and Me. The Skills of Communicating and Relating to Others* (California: Brooks/Cole Publishing Company, 1977), p. 211.
6. Ibid., p. 198.
7. Ibid., p. 137.
8. Barrie Hopson, 'Counselling and Helping' in David Griffiths (ed.) *Psychology and Medicine,* (Basingstoke: British Psychological Society and The Macmillan Press Ltd, 1981), p. 285.

7. Self-Awareness

> As helpers we should wisely remember that we are our
> own most important counselling instrument and that
> what we know and possess of ourselves makes a great
> difference in whether we help others effectively or not.[1]

If the counsellor is the constant in all counselling interactions, and if
we ourselves are our only 'tool', then it is of the utmost importance
that we are aware of our strengths and limitations, our effectiveness
and potential weaknesses, so that we can grow and improve in our
interactions. The importance of self-awareness and self-knowledge is
perhaps not stressed sufficiently, and it cannot be stressed too often.
Seeking to understand how we are likely to react in given situations
and to different people, and learning what triggers our emotional
responses gives us the opportunity to see what is preventing us from
achieving our ideal selves.

This learning about ourselves, our reactions, feelings, values, and
prejudices is an ongoing process, comparable to what we expect of
our clients. Using the attributes of genuineness, empathy, and
acceptance of the other person, and mindful of the essential
spontaneity of the counselling session, we afford for them an
opportunity to examine themselves, to recognise the need for
change, and we help them achieve this change. If we ourselves are
not also constantly changing, or open to change, then we will
become frozen in a single perspective.

Gerard Egan describes effective helpers thus:

> Ideally, they are first of all committed to their own growth – physical, intellectual, social-emotional, and spiritual ...[2]

This ongoing self-awareness, achieved through training and support from supervisors and colleagues, refreshes our counselling abilities and maintains our stability for others. Over-involvement with those we try to help in any area can result in a kind of emotional dust-bowl, where no matter how effective and accurate our assistance to those in trouble may be, there can come a time when we have no more to give. The phrase 'emotional burn-out' is used to describe this aridity which appears to be the result not only of over-involvement and failure to refresh our own resources, but also of the failure to recognise the effects of our work on ourselves.

> Training for counselling is not just a matter of developing a few new skills. It requires setting one's psychological house in order, so that one knows who he is and where he is going.[3]

Emotional responses
In chapter 5 we looked briefly at the necessity for the counsellor to be at home with her own feelings, in order to be able to cope with those of her client. If the counsellor is not aware of the 'triggers' which cause embarrassment, fear or anger in herself, then the expression of some topic or value by a client may throw her into a confusion of emotional reaction, which she may not even recognise. If loud voices and angry words frighten me, and if I have never looked at this reaction and the reasons for it, then sudden anger in a client and a raising of his voice may awaken this fear in me. My only way of dealing with it in the counselling situation may be to placate or deflect the anger. By indicating that his expression of it is unacceptable or threatening to me, I merely encourage him to bottle it up again. Alternatively, I may feel his rage is directed at me, and

automatically return it, and the result is merely a row. No exploration, no examination, just my customary emotional outburst: 'You have no right to speak to me like that', or angry defence: 'It's not part of my job to be insulted like that.'

Within families or at work, this type of response can become part and parcel of everyday reactions, with the same remarks triggering the same responses every time, and no one asking why. If we are prepared to own our feelings and to realise that our responses are only automatic because we do not look closely at them, then we can explore below their surface expression and realise that we have both the choice and the power to change our reactions. This ability not to be drawn in to the automatic stimulus-response which often governs our emotional dialogues helps us to cope with the expressed and unexpressed feelings of our clients. We become aware of how different feelings merge, and are empowered to encourage the free expression of feelings by others.

Values clarification

An important part of self-awareness is values clarification, which involves examining and clarifying our values and our reasons for behaving as we do. We often describe other people in terms of their value systems:

> I like her. She's very honest.
> He's a good neighbour, charitable and always willing to help.
> I'd vote for him; you could trust him with your life.

The values we hold reveal a great deal about the kind of people we are, and yet we often blindly adopt them from others, without really considering whether they match our actions or not. We may repeatedly proclaim that 'Honesty is the best policy' and without hesitation avail of goods which may have been stolen. Paying lip-service to values which we deny in our actions results in contradictory messages being given to those we come in contact with, and gives a blurred picture of us, both to ourselves and to others. Acting against deeply held values can lead to guilt, when in a vague and woolly way we feel guilty about some act done or undone, without quite knowing why. We are unable to use the feelings of unease to change our behaviour of tomorrow, because we do not understand the source of these feelings. If we are seeking change, then it is important that we know the *real* person we are, so that we may plan the person we wish to become.

To clarify and choose our own rules of conduct rather than accept them as well-worn childhood habits gives an ultimate freedom and power over our own decisions. If we have learned that a certain action is 'bad', and if we do not examine the reasons for ourselves, then we may live our lives either obeying rules which are no longer relevant, or reacting against standards of behaviour merely because they have been formulated by someone else. If I reiterate 'I should not or must not tell lies', then the rule or value is outside me, formulated and imposed by someone else. If I can say 'I want to be a truthful person because I believe lies to be harmful', then I have chosen the value of honesty freely, and I know why.

> Values, however, do not drive a man; they do not *push* him, but rather *pull* him ... Now, if I say man is *pulled* by values, what is implicitly referred to is the fact that there is always freedom involved: the freedom of man to make his choice ...[4]

In today's world, where values appear to be changing more rapidly than ever before, there is a choice for all of us when we are confronted with different standards: we can cling to the values of yesterday, we can switch to 'modern' values, or we can choose the standards by which *we* wish to live.

The idea of values clarification is sometimes understood as merely a wish to change old and treasured values because they are out of date and no longer relevant. However, the intention and the emphasis is on the word 'clarification' because if we can understand our reasons for holding certain values, then we can choose to adopt them as our own. We will be in a position to defend our value system when necessary, either to ourselves or to others, and we feel we are in charge of our own destinies. Alternatively we can live bounded by rules such as 'I ought to do this', and 'I should do the other'. We may feel helpless because we have not chosen these rules, and this helplessness can lead to anger against ourselves, against a family, a Church, a system. So anger and guilt, guilt and anger, can become an unhappy spiral, without any resulting change in behaviour. Examination and clarification of these standards and a resulting choice can lead either to a change in our behaviour or a change in our attitude towards ourselves.

For example, if I am feeling guilty about not visiting my aunt in hospital, I may constantly say: 'I should visit her. I haven't been for a week. I'm dreadful and I feel guilty.' I may say this several times a day, and continue to feel badly yet not go to the hospital. Perhaps I could find out precisely why I 'ought' to go. Is it because I like my aunt, and would like to comfort her, or because my relatives will think badly of me if I do not go? Is it because visiting the sick is a Christian act, or because if I do not go I will feel a failure as a caring person?

To look also at why I am *not* going can be useful, and my reasons can be very varied: laziness, no transport, genuinely too busy with my children's needs, my aunt was never kind to me, fear of hospitals and doctors, antagonism towards my aunt's family, etc. And here is where choice enters in, and a clarifying of my priorities. If I have concluded that I would like to see my aunt, but my children's immediate needs are pressing, then I can choose not to visit, but knowing why I have made that choice and understanding my reasons, I am free from guilt. On the other hand, I may weigh my chosen value of visiting the sick against my fear of hospitals, and make a clear choice to visit.

As counsellors, we afford our clients the opportunity to clarify their standards in a similar way. If they are to formulate and examine, and perhaps re-evaluate their values, it is important that we do not judge them, that we neither approve nor disapprove, for by doing so we impose outside standards on them once again. Counsellors 'must be able … to recognise the validity of different value systems'.[5] Tyler here uses the words 'recognise the validity', which does not imply either acceptance or rejection, merely *recognition*.

While we cannot suspend our own beliefs or values, we can suspend *expression* of these during counselling sessions. In this way we acknowledge the right of our clients to set standards of conduct for themselves, in the same way as we chose for ourselves, and we give them the time, the space, and the encouragement to do so. This kind of clarification is also important if a client sets herself a goal or a plan of action which is contrary to her basic, and perhaps unconscious, value system. Action resulting from poorly understood motives may cause conflict, and create new problems. The task of helping a client with this type of clarification is possible only if we have made sure that we are clear about our own values, lest we be waylaid by attitudes within ourselves of which we are not even aware.

Prejudices

> To be fully effective the counsellor needs a heightened awareness of his own inner life, including bodily feelings, emotional reactions, preferences, biases, hunches, and intuitions.[6]

Preconceived ideas about clients can colour our dealings with them and render it almost impossible to be objective. In counselling, the two people involved are equal as persons but their functions are totally different. The client by his very presence is subjective, while the counsellor strives all the time for objectivity. The client requires freedom from the currency of ordinary relationships, which exist through a sharing of feelings, ideas and problems, and looks for space to concentrate on his own difficulties.

We can be prejudiced either for or against a client, depending on how he matches our set notions, and if we are not aware of these prejudices in ourselves, then they act as blinkers on our understanding. Being aware of our learned stances towards people and circumstances gives us insight into how we could react towards a client. If we have a strong aversion to sexual abuse of children, then we may find it extremely difficult to work with a sexual offender in a dispassionate way. If we have never acknowledged to ourselves, and examined and explored our aversion, then we may find it impossible to be objective. Similarly, we may find it difficult to be objective with a client who discloses that we have a mutual friend, which may invest her with a 'halo' image, and equally cloud our accurate hearing of her difficulties. Recognition of these prejudices will lessen their impact, and learning about how we automatically sift client information through our background reflections is an essential part of self-awareness. Tiredness or preoccupation with our own worries can also act as a screen, making us less sensitive to our clients' needs.

The counsellor must be aware of the attitudes of his clients towards him. One person may feel antagonistic towards him because he reminds him of a feared teacher, or a client who is seeking to replace one crutch with another may feel over-dependent on the counsellor. Sometimes the delicate nature of the inter-dependencies of the counselling relationship may be even more complicated.

> A woman counsellor who reminds a boy of his mother may realise that she has in fact found him an exceptionally appealing boy and may have been showing tendencies either to protect him or to manage him.[7]

Recognition of such a tendency is usually sufficient either to offset it or lessen its impact.

PERSONAL RESPONSIBILITY

Any relationship between two people influences both, and the counselling relationship is no exception. It is for the counsellor to grasp what Kennedy calls the 'transactional essence' of the relationship, this two-way influence, because the client is usually in no position to be aware of it. The counsellor will not remain uninvolved or unaffected but will be alert to her own reactions, listening to her own responses, and constantly aware of the impact of this real and growing alliance on both herself and on her client. If she does not, then she will see the client as operating at a remove, and will miss some of the richest outcomes of counselling.

The personal responsibility of the counsellor is twofold. She is responsible for structuring and facilitating the climate within which the client can achieve the desired change, but she is also responsible for learning to know herself, becoming aware of her feelings and reactions, and changing where change is necessary. This includes becoming aware of herself in each counselling relationship, and acknowledging her reasons for being in this relationship.

> Before seriously considering herself a counsellor, each person should critically and honestly examine her own motivations for taking on the responsibilities of helping another person. Very simply, she should ask herself: 'What do I expect from the relationship? What will be my satisfactions and rewards in helping others?'[8]

This aspect of knowing why we have chosen to act in a counselling role is dealt with more fully in chapter 9.

PRACTICAL CHANGE

The question must arise as to how to achieve all this awareness of self, of motivation and prejudices. Knowledge of ourselves can perhaps best be achieved through a judicious mixture of introspection and disclosure coupled with feedback from others. 'Johari's Window'[9] (below) illustrates this process effectively. It shows four areas within ourselves, in varying stages of availability to our awareness.

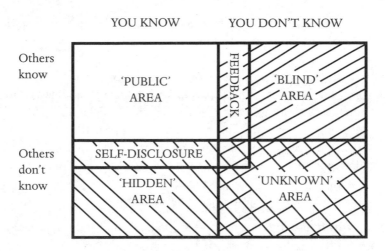

By sharing the area known to us, but not to others ('hidden area') by self-disclosure in group work, for example, we can lessen the 'blind' area, thus increasing our self-knowledge. The shrinking of the 'blind' and the 'hidden' areas in turn reduces the 'unknown' area. Thus external information, matched with our own insights, results in new awareness. By revealing more of ourselves and availing of other people's perceptions, our self-knowledge increases.

It is also possible to increase our self-awareness through self-exploration, using some of the stepping-stones of the counselling process. For example, if we become aware of stress signals in our lives, we can focus on ourselves as we would on the problems of a client.

1. We can take time, perhaps an hour twice a week, to examine closely the area causing stress, highlighting for ourselves the more sensitive aspects.

2. We can then try to discover the reasons for the distress by asking ourselves questions:
   - If so, how long has it been an irritant, and has it been increasing lately?
   - What are the triggers (times, people, situations) that cause it?

- Is the emotional reaction the real response or am I masking one emotion with another?

3. Having found a possible reason, it is important to spend some time checking it out. A reason that appears valid today may appear quite foolish tomorrow, and may also be only a partial reason, itself part of the distressful situation. If the cause is a circumstance or person, examining our reaction to them may highlight clues as to just why our reaction is thus. The need may not be to change the circumstances but to try to modify or transform our reaction, once it has been identified.

4. Finally, time spent investigating different solutions is most valuable, whether these be action or non-action, acceptance or avoidance. Finding the causes is never sufficient in itself. It is what we do with our new knowledge that is effective, and setting realistic and verifiable goals for ourselves is essential. We each, therefore, have potential for change, and also the responsibility to use that potential. To learn more about ourselves and to say complacently 'I cannot change – that's the kind of person I am' is not what we expect from our clients, nor should it satisfy us within ourselves. The responsibility for continual development is firmly in our own hands as counsellors.

NOTES

1. Eugene Kennedy, *On Becoming a Counsellor* (Dublin: Gill & Macmillian, 1977), p. 8.
2. Gerard Egan, *The Skilled Helper* (California: Brooks/Cole Publishing Company, 2nd edition, 1982), p. 26.
3. Leona E. Tyler, *The Work of the Counselor* (New Jersey: Appleton-Century-Crofts, 1983), p. 37.
4. Viktor E. Frankl, *Man's Search for Meaning* (New York: Pocket Books, 1963), pp. 157–8.
5. Leona E. Tyler, op. cit., p. 201.
6. E.A. Munro, R.J. Manthei and J.J. Small, *Counselling, a Skills Approach* (New Zealand: Methuen, 1983), p. 16.
7. Leona E. Tyler, op. cit., p. 160.
8. E.A. Munro et al., op. cit., p. 19.
9. 'Johari's Window' taken from J. Luft and H. Ingham, *The Johari Window: A Graphic Model for Interpersonal Relations* (California: University of Los Angeles, 1955).

8. Counselling with a Different Focus

TIME-LIMITED OR BRIEF COUNSELLING

Traditionally it has been believed that therapy will take as much time as each individual requires, and that it is often a comparatively lengthy process. Time-limited counselling attempts to pre-determine the time required and is often goal-focused. It is open to the charge that short-term therapy produces short-term changes only, but counsellors working in this way are usually aware that at times further, deeper work may be in the client's interests, and will suggest this.

Generally these 'time-sensitive' approaches emphasise the strengths and competencies of clients, and are often concerned with the solution or management of problems. The counsellor may be more active, more challenging and more directive, as brief therapy requires that the client be motivated towards solutions, and capable of being focused on immediate positive change and outcome. The emphasis is on the identification and the resolving of problems areas, rather than on the exploration of these. It is a future-focused way of working where the client becomes aware of obstacles to future happiness or effectiveness, and works with the counsellor to find ways of surmounting these within a short time-frame.

There are both supporters and critics of this way of working, but it is important that counsellors remain open to both the shortcomings and the benefits of different forms of therapy. The acknowledgement of the value of counselling, coupled with the increasing demand for its provision, has led to a need to spread scarce resources over a wider section of the population. Employee assistance programmes (EAPs) have dramatically expanded in industrial and commercial settings, many doctors and social services advocate brief counselling work, and the law courts are increasingly encouraging a set number of therapy sessions as part of bail or probation conditions.

Time-limited counselling is not merely a truncated form of counselling, and it cannot be merely defined in terms of time spent with clients, or in the number of sessions planned. It has a definite focus (the primary cause of concern identified by the client), a particular way of working (setting goals and exploring ways of achieving these goals), and an evaluation of progress and putting strategies in place for coping in the future. As in any setting, perhaps a note of caution needs to be sounded when the reason for using a particular way of working is an economic one, as there could be a danger that the needs and expectations of those paying the bills (the employers) might take precedence over the needs of the consumer (the client). However, perhaps, the very obviousness of this possibility is the greatest protection against its occurrence!

A FURTHER DIMENSION

The emphasis so far has been on one-to-one counselling with individual clients, but there are two areas which demand somewhat different techniques from the counsellor. While employing the same skills and requiring the same attributes, a further dimension of counselling is required, as the needs and demands of clients vary. Two of these areas are considered here, the first being group counselling, where the counsellor acts as facilitator for more than one person. The group at times takes over the role of the counsellor, focusing and listening in a less refined, exact way, but still helping to resolve problem areas, interacting within itself and with its members, as well as with the counsellor. The second area is crisis counselling, where the pace and tempo of the interchange is speeded up, and the need for action or instant decisions catapults the counsellor into a more forceful and directive role than may be her usual style.

GROUP COUNSELLING

Of its very nature, group counselling is different from individual counselling. The dialogue between two people becomes expanded to include different kinds of interaction, and the group members shift in and out of participating and observing roles. The atmosphere can be more threatening, as the participant faces not just a tolerant and understanding counsellor, but a group of equally anxious people, less attuned to the needs of others and less aware of their fragile defences. The client risks herself with an individual counsellor, but much more with a group who are all focused on themselves, especially in the initial stages. While the participant has the choice and the freedom to come or to go, to speak or to remain silent, the pace and content of the sessions are not fully within her power.

Purpose of group counselling

The convener or facilitator of a group needs to be very specific about the aims and objectives of the group, for herself and for the group members. For example, there may be discontent and dissent within a group if some members believe they are going to discuss the impact of TV programmes on their young families, and find in the course of group work that the real topic for other members is how to run a play-group in their area. Participants hope that group interaction will help them attain their personal objectives. A group can be formed to help its members survive and grow through a life crisis, with support from others caught in the same situation (HIV-positive group, separated people's group), or it can exist to help members grow and learn life skills (assertiveness training and social skills groups). Groups can be merely informational, where their purpose is to disseminate available facts about a specific topic, or they can be supportive towards a common aim, such as a weight watchers' club.

A therapy group is very different, as its aim is to explore, to change, to challenge, and be challenged towards personal growth. This kind of therapy group work is now part of most professional training courses for counsellors.

Structure of a group

A group working together with a shared aim is never merely a collection of individuals with their own responses and reactions. Stronger than the sum of its parts, every group forms itself into a whole, a unit with its own strengths and weaknesses. No two are ever the same, and while experience can teach some of the possible patterns and developments of groups, it cannot prepare the facilitator for all that may happen in the sessions. As a counsellor meets each new client in a particular and unique counselling relationship, in the same way each group is encountered for the first and only time.

Every member brings unique experiences and insights, and a successful group will tap the ideas and the expertise of each, combining the differing abilities in colourful patterns. The group becomes an entity able to deal with the difficult members: the 'bossy boots' who feels the need to direct everyone and organise every step; the silent member, who appears at every meeting and seems to be getting value, yet never contributes; the story-teller who has an anecdote to cover all situations; the parent who brings her family into every discussion. Indeed, a member looked on as 'difficult' by the group facilitator may prove both interesting and helpful to some other members of the group, and a source of learning to them. Intervention to deflect this difficult member might have interrupted and pre-empted the ability of the group as an entity to work through and beyond its individual differences.

Advantages of group counselling

The work of a group encompasses many of the same features as individual counselling: establishing a relationship, listening carefully to each person, assessing, focusing on and clarifying what has been said, seeking the meaning at the core of each statement, planning for change, all the components of individual counselling are there. The quality of the listening may not be as good, but more people are listening. The search for meaning beneath the words may not be as accurate, but the responses from so many different perspectives and experiences offer many interpretations.

Groups with experience shared by the members, such as bereavement groups, offer a common language and a fuller understanding of emotions and stages of development. If the aim of the individual is change and self-growth in some area, then self-knowledge is essential before change can take place. When we can see just where our dissatisfaction with the present state of affairs lies, then we can plan how we would like it to be, and what changes are necessary. Knowledge about ourselves can be gained by allowing others to see some hidden part of us and, by accepting their reaction as reflection, we begin to glimpse how they see us. Participation in a group carries a risk, as does all counselling, because we need to seek honestly the opinion of others, who in turn take the risk of honestly reflecting back how an action or statement of ours appeared to them. The support of group members for one another, through painful explorations of self, can be the strongest reason for participation. Why do we get angry with what someone else has said, and do we acknowledge that anger? Are we afraid of confrontation? Does a cheerful participant irritate us when we have something sad to share with the group? As social beings, many of our living difficulties arise from social contacts and structures, and increasing our awareness of how we deal with these in the apparently artificial, but nevertheless real atmosphere of a group can help us change and modify, or at least understand, our roles. Teaching social skills, or practising public speaking, will be more effective in a group since that is in itself a social setting.

Role of the facilitator
Where a counsellor has the role of group facilitator, it is important that he have some experience of working within groups himself, and some theoretical knowledge of their functioning. As a client will slowly come to trust a counsellor, and as the relationship between client and counsellor develops and changes, so the relationships within a group shift and grow. Standing back and watching the interplay of the group is not sufficient. All the basic counselling skills of understanding and focusing, highlighting and interpreting are fully used in the group setting, with the emphasis on the good of the

group rather than on the enhancement of the facilitator. While the general responsibility for action and interaction lies with each individual member, and with the group itself, the facilitator also has a responsibility to be aware of what is going on beneath the surface, the emotional under- and overtones, both within himself and each group member. Alert to signs of distress or anger, expressed or not, he needs also to be conscious of his own feelings and reactions towards other group members.

Direct intervention by the facilitator may be necessary where the group is backing away from a member who is visibly unhappy, endeavouring to ignore her pain, unnoticing in the hope that she will desist. Drawing attention to the embarrassment of the group, querying its function while giving the distressed person the space and caring supports to deal with her difficulty there and then, highlights the group reaction and prevents it from forcing the unhappy member to seal off her unhappiness and ignore it.

When hostility between some group members threatens to disrupt the group, intervention may shed light on what is happening, what hidden agenda is being used. The need here is not to tidy over the hostility, but to focus on it objectively, and ask the combatants to clarify, for themselves and for the group, the reasons for their anger.

Sometimes a group member will challenge or criticise the facilitator. Taking up the challenge can result in a trial of strength, in which there can be no winners, and the losers are both the group members and the facilitator. Entering into debate and putting the individual down may give some personal satisfaction, but the result is rarely helpful to the basic important aim: the good of the group and each of its members. The likelihood is that the group will lose both its direction and its impetus. For example, if the facilitator is seen as a figure of power and authority, the challenge may be a test to discover how much frank and honest discussion is possible within the group. If the facilitator reacts to the criticism with a hurt or punishing response, then the message could be that honesty and, therefore, effectiveness are not possible. However, the criticism could also give the facilitator the opportunity to dispel the authority image, perhaps by offering the criticism to the group for discussion. There may be no consensus as to whether the criticism was justified or not, but the debate engendered will often lead the group to a wider perspective, which could not have been reached without the first frank exchange.

Alternatively, the challenge could have arisen from the insecurity of a group member who was feeling the need to be seen as a forceful participant. The reasons behind any such challenge or criticism are rarely simple, but exploring them is more likely to lead to a satisfactory outcome than will merely ignoring or denying them and hoping they will go away.

While a group can produce considerable self-change and development for its members, initial participation can be tentative and slow. Allowing members to initially maintain defences and façades, and to emerge at their own pace, is important, especially with a person who is new to group work. Pushing someone to participate at a deep level, in the belief that drama and tears are necessary for progress, can lead to disintegration of a group or disturbance of the members. As in individual counselling, the facilitator will emphasise and highlight the strengths rather than the weaknesses of the members. Where a group is too large or the members appear unusually tentative, breaking into smaller groupings for initial discussions can be valuable. Three or four people can be less threatening than fifteen, and the confidence gained in the smaller group can be expanded when the larger group is re-established. While the facilitator will be able only to 'visit' each group, continually coming back into the larger unit for discussion and 'regrouping' can keep him in constant touch with each participant.

Ending a group
A group will develop through different stages towards the achievement of its objectives. Members will have participated in a learning situation, and each will bring both a different aspect of the experience and a different measure of learning away from the group.

> ... the helper needs to examine the progress of the group as a group in just the same way as a parent examines the progress of a child through various stages of development.[1]

It can be difficult for a member to move away from the accustomed protection of a group, and it is generally easier if this is done gradually rather than abruptly. For an individual, leaving a group which is still in existence can be comparable to a client separating from a one-to-one counselling relationship. When the planned life of a group, for example twelve sessions or twelve months, is ended, some members will opt for future friendly meetings, because the strength experienced in the group will often mean that participants are reluctant to allow this shared support to end. It is the job of the facilitator to be aware of the feelings aroused by the ending of a group and allow full discussion of these.

CRISIS COUNSELLING

Many counsellors or helpers who would never consider themselves to be crisis counsellors will nevertheless from time to time be faced with a crisis situation. Many of us meet crisis situations in our own lives, in our families, or on the street, and show a remarkable ability to manage the sudden and the unexpected. We react with the correct responses and can say afterwards, 'I managed that quite well'. However, having to consider how we would react to a crisis tomorrow, as a perceived 'expert', can be more frightening. We feel in advance the weight of responsibility for the correct handling of the situation, and the imagined impact of someone 'out of control' forcing us to take charge and *do* something. What do we mean by a crisis situation?

Causes of crises

Certain events or life-happenings have within them the potential for crisis. These are stressful events which can become crises, depending on the response of the individual. For convenience, we divide them here into two categories:

1. Developmental changes within a person's life, the 'passages' referred to by Gail Sheehy.[2] The movement from one stage of development to another can cause emotional uncertainty and disturbance, bringing as it does the need for change. These passages include going to school, adolescence, marriage, becoming a parent, old age; all normal and expected life events, but because of their transitional and demanding nature, they become times of potential stress.

2. The second category of events that can precipitate a crisis consists, not of inevitable changes, but of probable life events for us all, including bereavement, illness, exam failures, relationship difficulties. (We can include here also events that are not probable, but definitely *possible* in today's society, such as burglary, assault, rape, accidents.)

The first category suggests a more ongoing type of threat or difficulty, where the tenor and direction of the person's life is altering and will need to be dealt with over a period of weeks or months, but which can, with the addition of perhaps a single new factor, become a crisis point. The second category has more of the notion of now, of suddenness and urgency within the experience itself. No two people will react to any of these events in the same way, and what is manageable change for one may result in crisis for another. The crisis lies in the person's perception of and reaction to the event, rather than in the event itself. When the two categories coincide within a person's life – when an exam is failed during the difficulties of adolescence, or a mother dies while her daughter is coping with the stress of becoming a parent herself – then the possibility of crisis reaction increases. Dixon defines crisis as:

> ... a functionally debilitating mental state resulting from the individual's reaction to some event perceived to be so dangerous that it leaves him or her feeling helpless and unable to cope effectively by usual methods.[3]

Crises, therefore, of their nature are sudden, either a reaction to an unexpected happening, or precipitated by a 'last straw' event from a slow-building stressful state of affairs. For example, whether it be a case of attempted rape or failure in an exam, the person involved may find the situation beyond her normal control or coping skills; it becomes a time of suspense and danger, and there is a crisis. The 'blind panic' of crisis means that beyond this moment of fear, there is nothing. The task of the counsellor is to help her client through the physical reactions and on towards possibilities, alternatives, hopes.

The behaviours which confront the crisis counsellor can include bizarre behaviour, terror, attempted suicide.[4] While critical situations such as assault, burglary, or separation cause stress in all individuals, in many they cause manageable stress – the person manages to cope reasonably well with the anxiety. It is when the level of stress increases beyond the individual's coping capacity that the crisis occurs. The point of focus for the counsellor is the client's *perception* of the event, for it is here that the crisis lies, not in the precipitating event nor in the resulting behaviour.

If, as counsellors and helpers, we see the crisis merely within the event, then our reactions may be out of proportion or out of accord with our clients, and we may even create a crisis where none exists. If we allow our own feelings about, for example, being assaulted to flood a girl seeking help, then her own coping resources, which might have been able to deal with the event, risk being drowned by our horrified reactions. She will believe that she *must* be shattered, that of necessity she *will* suffer some enormous consequence, and we may force her into a crisis. As with general counselling, it is important to stay with the client and with her perception of the event.

Crisis theory

The recognition of the nature of crisis and methods of dealing with people in crisis, and the formulation of a working theory on the subject began with Lindemann (1944)[5] and was developed by Caplan (1964).[6] Caplan considers people to be generally in a state of balance, using familiar patterns of behaviour to interact with their world, to solve minor problems, and to cope with tension and stress. Different life problems may tilt the balance from time to time, but using the strategies for managing which have proved effective in the past, the individual returns more or less to equilibrium.

However, if a situation occurs within which his normal patterns of behaviour are not effective either in resolving the conflict or in returning him to balance, and the unfamiliar state of affairs does not appear amenable to any action on his part, then the emotional disturbance caused by this failure can herald crisis. While the actual events or circumstances may not appear to the onlooker to be particularly serious in themselves, the *reaction* of the person to the events is what will provoke the crisis.

Caplan saw the response of the individual as being a four-stage process. At first he attempts to use normal problem-solving patterns of behaviour in response to the crisis. The second stage is when it is becoming increasingly obvious that the coping attempts are not succeeding, and the tension and stress are increasing. At the third stage the individual reaches a point where he is forced to look for new behaviour patterns, perhaps with external help. He may walk away from the problem, or he may be helped to see it in a new light, with possible different outcomes. But if this third stage does not work, if the problem will not go away and cannot be resolved, then 'major personality disorganisation occurs and the individual may become psychotic, withdraw, suicide or just give up'.[7]

From this crisis theory has grown a system of crisis intervention, which Brockopp termed 'a social behaviour crisis counselling'.[8] This form of counselling deals with people now, and focuses on their coping abilities. It does not consider illness versus health, nor the previous problems of the client, but emphasises their strengths, resources, and social networks. It encourages a directive role by the helper, attempting to solve the immediate problem, and through information-giving and discussion, helping the client to change his approach to life, his lifestyle, and his interaction with his environment. 'The psychotherapist is empathetic but directive in definition of help offered, identifying the immediate problem and arresting further regression, as well as helping the person define resources and actions available.'[9] The emphasis is on dealing with the person within his community, rather than hospitalising or isolating him.

Thus, the very crisis experience can be used as a means of growth or development. In time of crisis, the heightened awareness of the individual and the fact that he has been jostled out of his customary ways of thinking and acting, render him more open to learning new coping skills and ways of managing his life.

> The fact that the new equilibrium is not necessarily the same as the old is precisely the quality which gives crisis its potential for growth.[10]

The helper's concentration on the strengths and resources of her client help him to appraise the crisis even more realistically, to see how it can teach him to deal with difficulties in the future, and, perhaps, how to help others through anxious events. The result can be a positive step forward in the client's development as a person, and the seeking of help at this time should be highlighted as a sign of strength and wisdom rather than as a sign of weakness.

What the helper can do

1. Perhaps the most important thing a helper can do is to remain calm. While this sounds self-evident, if the counsellor is overcome by the size, complexity and immediacy of the situation, then the help he can offer will be minimal. However, by absorbing the panic and 'grounding' the distress, the counsellor can be a stabilising presence for the client in the midst of chaos. This calmness, according to Kennedy, will 'reduce the impact of the crisis event',[11] and make possible the beginning of response demanded by the crisis. Crisis cannot be postponed or put aside. It is present *now*, and demands a response *now*. Not being drawn into the funnel of concentrated stress leaves the counsellor sufficiently detached to take charge and advise. The complete breakdown of coping skills means that self-responsibility is being

handed to somebody else; in the short term the counsellor may have to take decisions necessary to halt the process of disintegration, and begin to prepare space for the re-establishment of coping. Believing in the full responsibility of a person for themselves does not mean that we wait for their permission before cutting them free from a crashed car!

This willingness to become a decision-maker for others, recognising the crisis element and moving to meet it, can be difficult for a helper who normally operates as a non-directive counsellor. It demands that the counsellor takes temporary responsibility for another, in the belief that he is not at this moment capable of mobilising his own resources to act for himself. 'Nothing succeeds in an emergency like self-assurance',[12] and for many people in crisis, a helper who can calmly and confidently take charge lessens the impact of the crisis, and lays the foundations for the return of his coping skills.

2. The second step for the helper is an awareness of the physical response of the person, or the physical surroundings in which the crisis takes place. If the helper is faced with an attempted suicide, or excessive drink or drugs, then medical care may be the immediate step. The physical symptoms of acute stress or a lesser panic attack can be like those of a person in shock. Very basic actions such as ensuring warmth, providing a cup of hot sweet tea, an arm for them to cling to while they try to recoup, can be of value as introductory measures. Relaxation and breathing exercises may then restore a person to a point where they can begin to evaluate the situation.

3. It is important that the counsellor focus on the immediate crisis at the beginning. Trying to find out what triggered the disintegration will come next, but the focus at first needs to be on the feelings and confused helplessness of the person; to stifle expression of feelings or offer useless reassurances will be to no avail. The client is aware of being in a crisis, and of being immobilised by an event greater than her capacity to handle it. In

due course, discussion of this event in more manageable stages, as a series of smaller happenings leading to crisis, will lessen the effect of being overpowered and helpless.

4. From this discussion will come some indication of what triggered the crisis, or the event that appears to have started the panic. All our counselling skills of listening and observing will be needed here, because it is not the actual occurrence that is so important, but the client's perception of it. Often the actual event may seem trivial to us and the reaction irrational, as for example the attempted suicide of a teenager because of failure in what appears to us to be a relatively unimportant exam. But exam success may have been a ray of hope after successive failures in other areas; perhaps it was looked on as answering the expectations of others; future career hopes may have been bound into the passing of this exam. Whatever the reasons, they were sufficiently important to drive someone to the edge of self-destruction and the complete loss of ability to cope with life. This loss of coping skills is both the cause and the result of the crisis and, without help, can result in a vicious circle. Inability to keep going was part of the precipitating factor, and the recognition of this inability fuelled and intensified the problem as it got larger and larger. Through the confusion of emotional discharge, hopelessness and panic, the helper tries to glimpse the background to the crisis, because it is from this background that she will find pointers to future action, to restoration of coping ability once the acute phase of the crisis has passed.

5. The person in crisis is seldom in total isolation. Most people are part of some social network, like family, friends, workmates. While it is often true that the cause of the crisis originates within these social settings, it is also within these areas that the helper can usually mobilise some help and support. The person in crisis may have been brought for help by a significant person in his life, and that person can be useful in providing valuable information about the background and resources of the client. While

hospitalisation is sometimes necessary for a person in crisis, such transference to an unfamiliar environment can add new stresses to an already overburdened personal system. Seeking assistance from familiar contacts at home or at work can enable the client to regain control of his ability to deal with his environment. Once balance is restored, he may wish to learn some new coping skills to avoid recurrence of a crisis, and might be better able to adopt new behaviour patterns in familiar surroundings.

6. Throughout the crisis the client has lost control of his ability to cope with what is going on around him and within him, and these nightmare feelings are compounded if other people concur with the hopelessness. False optimism is useful to no one, but if the counsellor can convey his belief that the crisis stage is transient, and that the ability to cope will return, then this gives the client hope. He may not be able to see or believe in such an outcome, but the fact that someone else does, and communicates that belief to him, allows a *possibility* of hope even though the probability may seem as distant as before. Describing his management of a crisis situation, John Davis claimed: '... the fact that I could entertain hope for her was perhaps very important in that it enabled her to entertain hope for herself.'[13] This hope is easier for the counsellor who remembers that there is neither a simple correct answer, nor a perfect solution. What we can believe is that the client can be restored to a form of balance, like a spirit-level, from which point he can move forward towards plans and future action. The solution of the crisis and the longer-term outcome are both within the capacity of the client. He has coped until now, and he will regain these coping skills and learn new ones, and move back to a position of self-responsibility.

7. The crisis stage is short-lived by its very nature, and 'In most cases a crisis is resolved within four to six weeks'.[14] If the situation is continuous, then it is not a crisis as discussed here. While we as helpers are often not expected to continue with long-term counselling after a crisis, the relationship can develop into helping

over a longer period. Then, however, the nature of the counselling will change back to what was described earlier. If the person has regained her self-responsibility, the counsellor will step back in recognition of this. However, if our role as short-term helpers or rescuers has proved insufficient, the client may fail to regain coping skills, and the weight of stress may remain too great for the individual's capacity to deal with it. In this case, medical or psychiatric help may be necessary to prevent the person reaching a stage of major personality disorganisation, and it is essential that counsellors know where to refer these clients or at least where to make suitable enquiries for help.

Within this picture of crisis counselling, the importance of the counsellor's self-awareness is obviously even greater than for less urgent counselling, as we are dealing with a heightened and more intense state of distress in the client. We may be inherently reluctant to deal with crises, and may find that our reactions are to distance the event and delay involvement until someone else's help can be enlisted. But 'by their very nature, crises wait for no one',[15] and although a counsellor may feel relatively unskilled in the treatment of any such emergency, she may be the only person available. It is therefore important to have some knowledge of the nature of crises, where and how they are likely to arise, and to have looked at the basic steps for resolving them. Concern and kindness may not in themselves be sufficient, but as helpers used to mobilising the strengths of others in difficulty, our skills can be adapted in an emergency situation.

> The client in crisis needs above all else to know that his feelings are received and understood, and that he is being taken with the utmost seriousness ... The experience of being deeply understood and the sense of companionship which springs from this are in themselves powerful antidotes to the overwhelming feelings of panic and powerlessness which can be the concomitants of crisis.[16]

Aware of our limitations, mindful of the lack of perfect solutions, and bearing in mind the available medical expertise, we can help as much as is in our power, knowing that we may be the only person available right now.

NOTES

1. Stephen Murgatroyd, *Counselling and Helping* (London: British Psychological Society and Methuen, 1985), p. 142.
2. Gail Sheehy, *Passages* (New York: Bantam Books, Inc., 1977).
3. Samuel L. Dixon, *Working with People in Crisis* (Ohio: Merrill Publishing Co., 1986), p. 10.
4. J.K.W. Morrice, *Crisis Intervention* (Oxford: Pergamon Press, 1976), p. 8.
5. E. Lindemann, 'Symptomatology and Management of Acute Grief' in *American Journal of Psychiatry*, September 1944, pp. 101–2.
6. G. Caplan, *Principles of Preventive Psychiatry* (New York: Basic Books, 1964).
7. David Lester and Gene W. Brockopp (eds), *Crisis Intervention and Counselling by Telephone* (Illinois: Charles C. Thomas, Publisher, 1973), p. 93.
8. Ibid., p. 95.
9. *Eisteach*, IACT Journal, article by Robert Allen Simons, 'The Suicidal Person and the Psychotherapist', Vol. 2, No. 2 (Autumn 1997), p. 25.
10. Stephen Murgatroyd, op. cit., p. 12.
11. Eugene Kennedy, *Crisis Counselling* (Dublin: Gill & Macmillan, 1981), p. 2.
12. Ibid., p. 3.
13. Windy Dryden, 'Commitment: The Price of Keeping Faith', interview with John Davis in *Therapists' Dilemmas* (London: Harper & Row, 1985), p. 48.
14. J.K.W. Morrice, op. cit., p. 22.
15. Eugene Kennedy, op. cit., p. 11.
16. Dave Mearns and Brian Thorne, *Person-Centred Counselling in Action*, 2nd edition (London: Sage, 1999), p. 117

9. Beyond Practical Issues

WHY ARE WE COUNSELLING?

There are areas in counselling which need to be considered and a personal course of action decided on before we are ready to take on the task of helping people in need. So far we have considered the practical skills of counselling and the counselling process, and the very real need to know ourselves and our reactions in order to be effective in our help. There are other issues which require consideration, affecting our counselling, our values, and our human response to our clients.

It is not enough therefore to look at *how* we are counselling. We also need to ask *why* we are counselling. If we do not find some affirmation of purpose, and if we are not getting any satisfaction from what we are doing, then it is unlikely that we will do it well. It will become a drudge, a chore. Brazier[1] suggests that while there is a basic need in us all for positive regard and love, there is an equally imperative need to love others, an 'intrinsic altruism' that finds expression in the helping professions, including counselling. Yalom echoes this idea when he suggests that the positive impact on many counsellors from their work (much of which consists of hearing graphic accounts of suffering and unhappiness) may be '... a by-product of altruistic behaviour'.[2] Our examination of motive will rarely uncover a clear-cut, altruistic response such as, 'I want to help people, and I am interested only in their welfare'. Our answers are more likely to be: 'I need to earn a living, and counselling is what I feel I can do well'; 'I am a nurse, and I think practical counselling skills will help direct my nursing to encompass the whole person'; 'I have been appointed as counsellor within my organisation, and I want to do it as well as I can'; 'Counselling is a growth area right now, and I'm going to see how I can fit in'. Awareness of why we are working in the counselling area enables us to be more honestly aware of our own motives, our own reactions, and the reasons for our emotional responses to different situations. This is the self-knowledge we consider important for our clients, as they struggle to see their way more clearly, and it is equally important for us as part of our counselling training.

So that we can fully explore and examine why we take upon ourselves this sometimes rewarding but so often painful and demanding responsibility, we might consider some of the following possible reasons which could influence us:

1. Some counsellors believe that they have a monopoly on knowing how the world should be organised, and how people should think and act. They feel that by entering into a counselling role, they will be able to influence others to think as they do.

2. The role of the counsellor offers scope to those who have power needs that they cannot satisfy in other ways. To be in a position where we can dispense advice and sympathy to those in deep distress and confusion could make us feel like a person of consequence, because undoubtedly a counsellor assumes great importance in the eyes of many clients.

3. Sometimes the counselling relationship is seen as a close and satisfying bond with other people, supplying warmth and friendship lacking in other situations. The counsellor may be satisfying her own needs, and this can be at the expense of the client, whose needs in turn take second place.

4. Individual counsellors may find themselves trained in a profession which involves the use of counselling skills, and may continue in this role as a means of earning a livelihood, partly because there is no visible alternative.

5. Many counsellors believe that counselling is something they do well and, having the skills to offer, they set themselves to meet the need of others to share and explore in a counselling situation.

There are, of course, many other reasons why people become counsellors, and indeed many of us will discover several of these elements within our own motivation. It is important for counsellors to examine their own motives, and be aware of the effect these will have on themselves and on their clients.

Counselling can be most satisfying when we see people changing, becoming more effective, learning to manage their lives, rising from depression and misery, and we see this resulting at least partly from our help. However, it can be only a small step from this satisfaction to a belief that we are in some way in control of distressed people, and that it is within our power to 'mould' or 'shape' others. We need to remain aware of the danger of becoming manipulators, believing that we know what is best for others.

People in trouble look for a helper on whose strength and encouragement they can rely. They naturally become dependent on the helper for a time, and are sometimes willing to invest her with wisdom and knowledge in great abundance. If we are not clear about our reasons for counselling, and our potential as helpers, then we could come to believe in these almost magical powers, instead of being aware of them as mere reflections from the current troubled perspective of our clients. We need to realise that our interventions are momentary and partial, serving mainly to illuminate dark areas, and acting as signposts at a confusing crossroads. If we want to be *always* an influence, then counselling will not satisfy our needs. 'Always' is a rare word in counselling, and sometimes the person we feel we helped most disappears from our lives, and we are disappointed that he does not keep in touch. Our role as counsellor is transient, and we can in no way live other people's lives for them, nor can we control how they live. Our role is to clarify, encourage choice of goals, and support these choices. The specific nature of this role needs to be understood and acknowledged both by ourselves and by our clients.

Further aspects of the responsibility of the counsellor include not being afraid to recognise our limitations, being confident enough to take responsibility for our part in a counselling session, and feeling free to acknowledge a mistake or misunderstanding if it occurs. Another test of our confidence both in ourselves and in our counselling skills is whether we can accept that while we may not be the most competent person in a particular situation, we may be the only person available, and assume responsibility accordingly.

LIMITATIONS

Exploration of why we are counselling helps us to become more aware of the limitations inherent in counselling. For example, to acknowledge in advance that I will make mistakes is to be aware of my fallibility and my constant need to learn and grow. These mistakes may range from interrupting my client in a thoughtless manner, to missing the signs that a client is on the verge of self-destroying behaviour, and my consideration of these errors can be either destructive or constructive. It would be destructive to focus totally on my mistake, playing and replaying the interview in my mind, wishing it might have been otherwise and remaining in the 'if only' aspect. Such blockage could damage my confidence as a helper.

On the other hand, analysing the error of speech or judgement, preferably with a colleague or supervisor, can help me to consider alternative strategies for the future, eliminate aspects of my helping role that were not useful, and generally make the occasion into an opportunity for growth in my counselling ability.

It is important also to be aware that I cannot be available to anyone, client or friend, all the time. I may have family commitments, holidays or illness, or I may decide to work within clearly defined time parameters, and once I have outlined these to my clients and to myself, then I operate within these. If I do not clarify these limits for myself, then I may agree to keep open house for a client when I really do not want to, putting stress on myself and my family with which we cannot cope, and perhaps feeling guilty if a client says, 'I rang, and you weren't there'. I need also to be aware in advance that there are some clients with whom I may not be compatible, with whom I may not be able to work effectively. The reasons for this may be within me, within the client, or independent of either of us, but the results will be the same. As counsellor and client, we may not 'suit', and the result may well be that I will try to refer the client on, or the client may choose not to come back. This can create difficulties if the lack of suitability is evident to either the counsellor or the client, but not to both. I need to be aware that if a client leaves, or simply fails to return, then it is not necessarily a reflection on my ability as a counsellor.

The detachment so essential for effective counselling will not be attainable all the time. I will inevitably feel angry occasionally with a client who is behaving towards somebody else in a seemingly cruel way, or impatient with someone who appears to move at a snail's pace towards her objective. Being aware of these reactions, examining them to discover their source, and learning to accept them without necessarily expressing them brings me to a further realisation that I am not a perfect counsellor. I have areas which need to be improved, and areas where I need to change. (The anger or impatience I feel rising within me at times can be acknowledged and placed aside with a mental note to deal with it later, as its expression right now would be both inappropriate and of no use to my client. This is not a suppression of emotions, because I allow them into my awareness, but it is a postponement of their examination and expression, and the important element here is to remember to give myself time later on to process the feeling aroused.)

I also try to remember that there are more effective counsellors than myself, who might be better able to deal with this particular client right now. There are always better, more articulate, kinder people, but at this moment this client is looking to me for help. I am the person available, I am here for this client, and I am prepared to do as well as I can. I cannot do more just now, and I cannot be someone else. I look at what I can do, recognising my limitations, and do my best.

THE ETHICAL NATURE OF COUNSELLING

> ... the primary role of the counsellor is not one of
> merely using techniques. It is essentially an ethical task.
> Simply stated, it is to serve the client's best interests.[3]

When we looked at self-revelation as a skill, one of the tests for efficacy was whether it was in the client's interests, or merely to serve some purpose or need to share within ourselves. We have emphasised responsibility for self, both on the part of the client and of the counsellor, but the counsellor must take responsibility for the movement from what Kennedy calls 'the abstract, diagnostic realm'.[4] It is the counsellor who arranges appointments, charts progress, monitors the time available, and in general lends her strength to the other. She has a responsibility to the client in areas of confidentiality, competence, possible referral, and remains aware of the ethical standards of the client. She is similarly responsible to society, remaining aware of the social codes and moral expectations of the community, lest clients unwittingly become involved in damaging personal conflicts or legal infringements. Indeed, Paul Halmos brings the ethical aspect of counselling a step further when he suggests that counselling may be the obvious 'secular inheritor of the pastoral function' which he perceives as being in decline for some years past.[5]

Whether or not we would agree with this, it is obvious that the client will often afford us access to hidden areas of his self, and we must be aware of our responsibility to respect this privileged insight. We need to be fully aware of how damaging our intervention could be if we are careless, and how we could find ourselves '... trampling on the sacred places of others' personalities in the process'.[6]

This ethical aspect of counselling is fully acknowledged by the Irish Association for Counselling and Psychotherapy. It has drawn up a Code of Ethics and Practice (see Appendix) for its members, which covers the need for integrity, confidentiality, and responsibility on the part of the counsellor, together with respect for the values and beliefs of the client, and underlines the idea that counselling is a deliberately undertaken responsibility.

This intentional nature of counselling, the placing of oneself in a role of responsibility, perceived as such by others, carries with it the duties of being responsible towards others, of becoming as effective as we are able, and of always acting in the best interests of our clients.

DESIRED OUTCOMES OF COUNSELLING

Helpers who look for happy endings or expect tidy solutions will be continually disappointed. The very nature of counselling is transient, designed to help the person in distress to regroup and reassess the situation, and make the best of the result. If our aim in counselling were merely one of problem-solving, then we could listen for a while, outline our perceived solution, and say 'next please'.

> The counsellor's function in this process is not to offer a solution to the client's problems, but to assist the client to see himself more clearly in all his positive, negative and contradictory aspects.[7]

The expectations of clients may often be quite different from our own, and it is very easy to impose our notion of what is in the best interests of a client and our ideas of progress.

If a client fails to return after one or two sessions, we will look closely in supervision at our part in the sessions, and if we measure success by our own expectations, we may feel we have failed somewhere. In fact, the client has exercised his self-responsibility by deciding not to return, and the reasons may vary from feeling that he can make the next step on his own, to deciding to look for someone who will unequivocally tell him what to do. We may never know, but the decision not to come back may have little to do with us, and may even be a sign of progress.

Success often means different things to the client and to the counsellor. The counsellor may be looking for a beginning, middle, and end to the story, while the client is more likely to be looking at counselling as a chapter in a book, which will fit into her life-story, and perhaps change its direction; its effectiveness will be judged by future events, about which the counsellor may never know.

For example, Anne was experiencing difficulties in her marriage, and eventually persuaded her husband, James, to come to a counsellor. James came reluctantly and in counselling he was unhelpful, unfeeling, wishing that she 'would sort herself out', as he saw no reason to change any aspect of their marriage. He felt that only Anne was dissatisfied. The two counselling sessions were a struggle between them, and the counsellor felt that no progress had been made, and no change effected. The counsellor here was assuming that the expectations of his first client, Anne, were that counselling would improve the quality of the marriage and make the relationship between herself and James happier and more constructive. In fact, it later became evident that Anne's expectations of the counselling experience had been fully realised. She wanted to prove to herself that James was intractable and immovable, even with a counsellor (who represented for her the world outside their marriage). Since James refused to change, or even to acknowledge that any change was desirable or necessary, Anne felt fully justified in leaving the marriage and seeking separation. Her expectations were fulfilled, and she looked on the outcome as 'successful' for her needs.

It can happen also that a client examines her situation with the counsellor, looks at options and different perspectives, and, having done so, chooses *not* to change. The idea of change, the effort involved, the resulting difference in lifestyle, may threaten her social network, and she may choose to remain in the situation as it is, behaving in the same way as before. This is her choice and her decision, though it may be difficult for the counsellor to accept this outcome. Remembering that the ultimate and shared aim of counselling is the redundancy of the counsellor, the counselling relationship deals not only with current difficulties, but teaches and empowers the client to make wise decisions in the future, to cope with crises which may arise. We are working with clients to enable them to help themselves in the future, but this aspect of the relationship may never become fully clear to the client, and may therefore not be part of her expectations.

CONFIDENTIALITY

In these days of computer memories and teamwork, the notion of confidentiality becomes both more important and more complex in its application. Of its nature, the client-counsellor relationship renders confidential any information imparted to the counsellor by the client. The theory of confidentiality is relatively easy to accept – but consider how we would act if the welfare or safety of a third person was at risk, or if part of the information was essential for hospital or school records, or for the personnel files of a company.

The need to examine our views on confidentiality, or the limits we have placed on it, may arise in respect of a particular person or situation. How might a counsellor respond to parents who initially urged their teenage daughter to come for counselling, are paying for the sessions, and now request a report on her progress? Would we think confidentiality had been breached in case discussion with colleagues, or in using case histories as illustrations within a teaching role? What are our personal guidelines for sharing information regarding a client who is also a patient in hospital, and whose doctors request information from her file?

Counsellors are currently debating issues such as mandatory reporting of child abuse, how records are kept and to whom they are available, whether information shared between counsellor and client is 'privileged' in law, the possible elasticity of confidentiality in group work or in supervision. If there are limits on total confidentiality, for whatever reason, it is of paramount importance that we make this clear to our clients at the outset.

> Confidentiality is a natural right of the client and is at the heart of the trust which is vital to the facilitation of the development of the individual ... Assurance to a client of the confidential nature of the counselling process, bounded by the above exceptions, facilitates the release of traumatic memory and opens out the potential for renewal and development.[8]

It is only possible to pose the general question here, for the particular decisions will have to be made by every counsellor. We need to decide whether we consider confidentiality to be absolute or not, and this is particularly relevant in a country with a small population, where the smallest indiscretion may lead to universal recognition of the person or case in question. It is the responsibility of every helper to decide in advance his or her stance on confidentiality, so that we do not make these decisions under the pressure of individual or critical cases. Our decision will be part of our personal philosophy of helping, made in relation to our own ethical standards and our work setting.

SUPPORT FOR THE COUNSELLOR

Being a counsellor can be a lonely occupation, and at times we can feel that the whole troubled world is coming to us for help. We risk becoming too closely involved and being weighed down by the burden of trust and dependence. Supervision is today considered an essential part of the professional life of a practising counsellor. It is no longer 'just for trainees'. It serves to focus the counsellor on an assessment of her work, and ensures that she is not operating in a vacuum, perhaps compounding and repeating unproductive ways of working, perhaps entirely missing some aspect of her client's experience. 'From the training supervision of beginning counsellors through to the collegial consultation of experienced practitioners, supervision is dedicated to helping clients by helping their counsellors.'[9]

The focus is on the client, filtered through the effect the client has on the counsellor. The relationship between the supervisor and the counsellor has many of the same qualities as that between client and counsellor, but it is of course not a therapeutic relationship. It offers support, critique, affirmation, and encouragement, accepts the fact that we can at times feel 'stuck', and challenges us to explore all aspects of our work.

Ongoing personal development, and staying in touch with new writing and theories in counselling help to keep our work from becoming routine and repetitive. Exchanging new ideas about counselling with other counsellors, sharing information on techniques or outcomes gleaned from a workshop or seminar both 'grounds' us and alerts us to developments in our area of work. Sharing knowledge makes us more aware of different levels of expertise, and connects us with colleagues to whom we may wish to refer clients with a specific difficulty. It is essential that we are continually learning and open to new ideas, because if we are not prepared to change and grow ourselves, we cannot in fairness expect our clients to do so.

NOTES

1. David Brazier (ed.) *Beyond Carl Rogers* (London: Constable, 1993), pp. 76–7.
2. Irvin Yalom, *Eisteach*, Winter 2004, p. 5.
3. E.A. Munro, R.J. Manthei and J.J. Small, *Counselling, A Skills Approach* (New Zealand: Methuen, 1983), p. 12.
4. Eugene Kennedy, *On Becoming a Counsellor* (Dublin: Gill & Macmillian, 1977), p. 25.
5. Paul Halmos, *The Faith of the Counsellors* (London: Constable, 1981 edition: first published 1965), p. 37.
6. Eugene Kennedy, op. cit., p. X.
7. Eleanor O'Leary, *The Psychology of Counselling*, (Cork: Cork University Press, 1982), p. 13.
8. *Eisteach*, IACT Journal, Vol. 2, No. 2 (Autumn 1997). Article by Patricia Kennedy, 'Confidentiality and the Counselling Profession', p. 15.
9. C. Feltham and W. Dryden, *Developing Counselling Supervision* (London: Sage, 1994), p. X.

Appendix: Irish Association for Counselling and Psychotherapy

Summary of Code of Ethics and Practice 2005

This summary is intended to convey the essence of the Code to members of the Association and the general public. It is not intended to replace the Code: for all formal purposes (for example, ethical decision-making or complaint against a member) reference should be made to the full Code.

Preamble

The first paragraph of the preamble defines counselling and psychotherapy as professional activities involving Association members, hereafter called practitioners, and their clients. The practitioner offers an impartial helping relationship which respects the client's personal values and autonomy. Practitioners recognise the importance of confidentiality in establishing such a relationship. Counselling and psychotherapy are formal activities involving an agreed contract. To maintain their effectiveness, practitioners review their work regularly in a confidential setting with a supervisor.

In joining the Association, members agree to comply with the provisions of the Code. The Code applies to their professional activities and any behaviour that might impinge on those.

To ensure that they behave in an ethical manner, practitioners are required to use a formal procedure in examining ethical aspects of their work. In situations where ethical decisions can be complex and difficult, and different ethical principles may be in conflict, the best decision comes from considering issues systematically.

Like all other citizens, practitioners are subject to the law, and their practice must conform to the law.

Content of the Code
The Code is based on four overall ethical principles, under which specific ethical standards are elaborated in greater detail.

Principle 1: Respect for the rights and dignity of the client
Practitioners are required to treat their clients as persons of intrinsic worth with a right to determine their own priorities, to respect clients' dignity, and to give due regard to their moral and cultural values. Practitioners take care not to intrude inappropriately on clients' privacy. They treat as confidential all information obtained in the course of their work. As far as possible, they ensure that clients understand and consent to whatever professional action they propose.

Principle 2: Competence
Practitioners are required to monitor and develop their professional skills and ethical awareness on an ongoing basis. They recognise that their expertise and capacity for work are limited, and take care not to exceed the limits.

Principle 3: Responsibility
In their professional activities, practitioners are required to act in a trustworthy and reputable manner towards clients and the community. They refer clients to colleagues and other professionals, as appropriate, to ensure the best service to clients. They act appropriately to resolve ethical dilemmas and conflicts of interest.

Principle 4: Integrity
Practitioners take steps to manage personal stress, maintain their own mental health, and ensure that their work is professionally supervised. They are required to be honest and accurate about their

qualifications and the effectiveness of the services which they offer. They treat others in a fair, open, and straightforward manner, honour professional commitments, and act to clarify any confusion about their role or responsibilities. They do not use the professional relationship to exploit clients, and they deal appropriately with personal conflicts of interest. They take action against harmful or unethical behaviour in colleagues.

Bibliography

ANDREWS, Paul, *Changing Children* (Dublin: Gill & Macmillan, 1994).

BASS, Ellen and DAVIS, Laura, *The Courage to Heal* (London: Cedar/Mandarin, 1992).

BERNE, Eric, *What do you do after you say Hello?* (London: Corgi Books, 1986).

BOYNE, Edward (ed.) *Psychotherapy in Ireland* (Dublin: Columba Press, 1993).

BRAZIER, David (ed.) *Beyond Carl Rogers* (London: Constable, 1993).

―――― *Zen Therapy* (London: Constable, 1995).

BROCKOPP, Gene W., 'Crisis Intervention: Theory, Process and Practice' in David Lister and Gene W. Brockopp (eds) *Crisis Intervention and Counseling by Telephone,* (Illinois: Charles C. Thomas, 1973).

CAPLAN, G., *Principles of Preventive Psychiatry* (New York: Basic Books, 1964).

CASEMENT, Patrick, *On Learning from the Patient* (London: Routledge, 1985).

―――― *Further Learning from the Patient* (London: Routledge, 1990).

DELROY, Sandra, in collaboration with GORDON, Cheryl, *Just Beneath the Surface – The Processes of Counselling and Psychotherapy* (London: Dobro Publishing, 1996).

DIXON, Samuel L., *Working with People in Crisis* (Ohio: Merrill Publishing Co., 1986; first published 1979 by C.V. Mosby Co.).

DRYDEN, Windy, *Therapists' Dilemmas* (London: Harper & Row, 1985).

EGAN, Gerard, *You and Me. The Skills of Communicating and Relating to Others* (California: Brooks/Cole Publishing Company, 1977).

—— *The Skilled Helper* (California: Brooks/Cole Publishing Co., 1982; first published 1975).

FELTHAM, Colin, *What is Counselling?* (London: Sage, 1995).

—— *Time-Limited Counselling* (London: Sage, 1997).

FELTHAM, Colin and DRYDEN, Windy, *Developing Counselling Supervision* (London: Sage, 1994).

—— *Dictionary of Counselling* (London: Whurr Publishers, 1993).

FRANKL, Viktor E., *Man's Search for Meaning* (London: Hodder and Stoughton, 1987).

GILMORE, Susan K., *The Counselor-in-Training*, Century Psychology Series (New Jersey: Prentice Hall, Inc., 1973).

GRIFFITHS, David (ed.) *Psychology and Medicine* (Basingstoke: British Psychological Society and The Macmillan Press Ltd, 1981).

HALMOS, Paul, *The Faith of the Counsellors* (London: Constable, 1981).

HARRIS, Thomas A., *I'm OK – You're OK* (London: Pan Books, 1973).

—— *Staying OK* (London: Pan Books, 1986).

HOWE, David, *On Being a Client,* (London: Sage, 1993).

INSKIPP, Francesca, *Skills Training for Counselling* (London: Cassell, 1996).

INSKIPP, Francesca and JOHNS, Hazel, *Principles of Counselling Series Part 1* (1983) and *Part II* (1985), audio tapes (Sussex: Alexia Publications).

IRISH ASSOCIATION FOR COUNSELLING AND PSYCHOTHERAPY, *Code of Ethics* (Dublin: IACP, 2005).

JACOBS, Michael, *Swift to Hear* (London: SPCK, 1985).

KENNEDY, Eugene, *Crisis Counselling* (Dublin: Gill & Macmillan, 1981).

KENNEDY, E. and CHARLES, S. C., *On Becoming a Counsellor* (Dublin: Gill & Macmillan, 2nd edition 1992).

KIRSCHENBAUM, H. and HENDERSON, V. I. (eds) *The Carl Rogers Reader* (London: Constable, 1990).

LAW, Bill, 'The Concept of Counselling (2)' in *Concepts of Counselling*, T.D. Vaughan (ed.) (London: Bedford Square Press, 1975), p. 80.

LINDEMAN, E., 'Symptomatology and Management of Acute Grief' in *American Journal of Psychiatry*, September 1944.

LINDSAY, Susan, *The Love Crucible* (Dublin: Marino, 1995).

LOUGHARY, J.W. and RIPLEY, T.M., *Helping Others Help Themselves* (New York: McGraw-Hill, 1979).

LUFT, J. and INGHAM H., *The Johari Window: A Graphic Model for Interpersonal Relations* (California: University of Los Angeles, 1955).

MASLOW, A.H., *The Farther Reaches of Human Nature* (Harmondsworth: Penguin Books, 1971).

MASSON, Jeffrey, *Against Therapy* (London: Collins, 1989).

McGUIRE, James and PRIESTLEY, Philip, *Learning to Help* (London: Tavistock Publications, 1983).

MAY, Rollo, *The Art of Counselling* (London: Condor Press/Souvenir, 1992).

MEARNS, Dave and Thorne, Brian, *Person-Centred Therapy Today* (London: Sage, 2000).

MORRICE, J.K.W., *Crisis Intervention* (Oxford: Pergamon Press, 1976).

MUNRO, E.A., MANTHEI, R.J. and SMALL, J.J., *Counselling, a Skills Approach* (New Zealand: Methuen, revised edition 1987).

—— *Counselling: The Skills of Problem-Solving* (London: Routledge, 1995).

MURGATROYD, Stephen, *Counselling and Helping* (London: British Psychological Society/Methuen, 1985).

MURGATROYD, Stephen and WOOLFE, Ray, *Coping with Crisis* (London: Harper & Row, 1982).

NELSON-JONES, Richard, *Personal Responsibility Counselling and Therapy: an Integrative Approach* (London: Harper & Row, 1984).

—— *Practical Counselling and Helping Skills* (London: Cassell, 3rd edition, 1993).

—— *The Theory and Practice of Counselling Psychology* (Eastbourne: Holt, Rinehart and Winston, 1982).

O'FARRELL, Ursula, *Courage to Change: The Counselling Process* (Dublin: Veritas, 1999).

—— *Considering Counselling* (Dublin: Veritas, 2004).

PALMER, Stephen and Varma, Ved (eds) *The Future of Counselling and Psychotherapy* (London: Sage, 1997).

PATTERSON, C.H., *Relationship Counseling and Psychotherapy* (New York: Harper & Row, 1974).

—— *Theories of Counseling and Psychotherapy* (New York: Harper & Row, 1980).

PROCTOR, Brigid, *Counselling Shop* (London: Burnett Books in association with André Deutsch Ltd, 1978).

ROGERS, Carl R., 'The necessary and sufficient conditions of therapeutic personality change' in *Journal of Consulting Psychology,* Vol. 21 (1957), p. 99.

ROGERS, Carl R., 'Characteristics of a Helping Relationship' in *Journal of Personnel Guidance,* Vol 37 (1958), pp. 6–16.

—— *Client-Centred Therapy* (London: Constable, 1995; first published 1951).

—— *A Way of Being* (New York: Houghton-Mifflin, 1986; first published 1980).

—— *On Becoming a Person. A Therapist's View of Psychotherapy* (London: Constable, 1986; first published 1967).

ROWE, Dorothy, *Depression: The Way Out of Your Prison* (London: Routledge, 1995).

SHEEHY, Gail, *Passages* (New York: Bantam Books Inc., 1977).

—— *Understanding Men's Passages* (New York: Random House, 1998).

STORR, Anthony, *The Art of Psychotherapy* (London: Butterworth Heinemann, 2nd edition, 1995).

THORNE, Brian, *Carl Rogers* (London: Sage, 1992).

—— *Person-Centred Counselling. Therapeutic and Spiritual Dimensions* (London: Whurr Publishers, 1996).

THORNE, Brian, and Lambers, Elke, *Person-Centred Therapy: A European Perspective* (London: Sage, 1998).

THORNE, Brian, and Mearns, Dave, *Person-Centred Therapy Today* (London: Sage, 2000).

TRUAX, Charles B. and CARKHUFF, Robert R., *Towards Effective Counseling and Psychotherapy: Training and Practice* (Chicago: Aldine Publishing Co., 1967).

TYLER, Leona E., *The Work of the Counselor* (New Jersey: Appleton-Century-Crofts, 1983), p. 99.

WILKINS, Paul, *Person-centred Counselling in Focus* (London: Sage, 2003).

WORDEN, J. William, *Grief Counselling and Grief Therapy* (London: Tavistock Publications, 1983).

YALOM, I. D., *Love's Executioner and Other Tales of Psychotherapy* (London: Penguin Psychology, 1991).

——— *The Gift of Therapy* (London: Piatkus, 2002).

ZOHAR, Danah, *The Quantum Self* (London: Bloomsbury, 1990).

See also:

Éisteach, Quarterly Journal of the Irish Association for Counselling and Psychotherapy, Dublin.

Developing Counselling Series: Series editor Windy Dryden (London: Sage, 1994).
Developing the Practice of Counselling, Windy Dryden and Colin Feltham.
Developing Counsellor Supervision, Colin Feltham and Windy Dryden.
Developing Counsellor Training, Windy Dryden and Colin Feltham.
Developing Person-Centred Counselling, Dave Mearns.
Developing Psychodynamic Counselling, Brendan McLaughlin.

Counselling in Action Series: Series editor Windy Dryden (London: Sage, 1996; first published 1991).
Eleven titles including:
Person-Centred Counselling in Action, Dave Mearns and Brian Thorne.
Psychodynamic Counselling in Action, Michael Jacobs.
Experiences of Counselling in Action, (eds) Dave Mearns and Windy Dryden.

Key Figures in Counselling and Psychotherapy Series: Series editor Windy Dryden (London: Sage, 1992).

Titles include:
Carl Rogers, Brian Thorne.
Eric Berne, Ian Stewart.
Sigmund Freud, Michael Jacobs.